Pink = good to come
back to

Yellow = ok to com
back to but not to
good

LET'S GO
Skating

ALEX TAYLOR

PARTRIDGE PRESS

LONDON · NEW YORK · TORONTO · SYDNEY · AUCKLAND

TRANSWORLD PUBLISHERS LTD
61-63 Uxbridge Road, London W5 5SA

TRANSWORLD PUBLISHERS (AUSTRALIA) PTY LTD
15-23 Helles Avenue, Moorebank, NSW 2170

TRANSWORLD PUBLISHERS (NZ) LTD
Cnr Moselle and Waipareira Aves,
Henderson, Auckland

Published 1991 by Partridge Press
a division of Transworld Publishers Ltd
Copyright © 1991 Alex Taylor

A catalogue record for this book
is available from the British Library

ISBN 185225 128X

Typeset in Baskerville by
Falcon Graphic Art Ltd.

Printed in Great Britain
by Biddles Ltd, Guildford and King's Lynn

Contents

1 *Introduction*

Ice skating is for everyone. Whatever your age, ice skating is enormous fun and terrific exercise and is now one of the fastest-growing sports in the United Kingdom. In fact there are now twice as many rinks as there were in the 1970s, so there has never been a better time to get your skates on!

Modern ice rinks have all the facilities that you would expect. The surroundings are generally good, along with the services they provide, so the patrons are able either to glide around in the best possible atmosphere, or watch in reasonable comfort.

The general standard of catering is high, so you can be sure of a good hot drink waiting for you when you step off the ice. For those who wish something a little stronger, there is bound to be a licensed bar on the premises.

Moving on to equipment, most ice rinks have a shop where you can purchase your boots, skates and accessories, along with experts available to help and guide you through any difficult decisions. All rinks in the United Kingdom have skate hire facilities where you can rent some equipment for the first few visits. (There is a comprehensive list of United Kingdom ice rinks and relevant contact addresses in the appendix at the back of this book.)

One of the most attractive aspects of the sport is the social side. You will find people of all age groups and skating standards and from all kinds of backgrounds and occupations. Bearing all this in mind, the ice rinks allocate specific general-skating and practice times for the kids and the grown ups according to their level of ice-skating expertise.

The same applies to the 'How to Skate' classes that they organize. The youngest children are allotted time when they can be taught the basics of the sport, in small groups. Here they will learn such essential moves as forward and backward skating, and, rather importantly, how to stop.

Most rinks run these 'Tiny Tots' sessions after school or during the weekend. Many of the greatest skaters have started their careers during these sessions, so if you have a child under the age of five, this is probably the best place to start.

A children's skating lesson

For those of you between five and fifteen years, the children's classes will be open. It is usual to base these classes on a Skating Association award scheme, so as to combine the achievement of a good rate of progress with learning an interesting range of moves. It is usual for the participants to undertake a set period of instruction, followed by a practice period.

This is also a good way of making your first skating friends and, as you advance, by way of gaining a relevant badge, you will be moved up into the next group, where you will learn ever more interesting moves, more often than not taking your new found skating friends with you.

The teenagers are drawn by the disco sessions along with superb lighting, fantastic sound systems and (in some rinks) giant video screens. These are great social events, with many opportunities to meet old friends and bump into a few new ones. If you fit into this age group, Saturday and Sunday afternoon and evening sessions are probably the best time for you. To be certain, call your local rink before you go.

For those of you who are over the age of fifteen there are the adult classes, where you can learn the basic moves with people of a similar age group and standard. These classes tend to be extremely popular, so get in touch with your ice rink as soon as possible if you wish to take part.

The adult classes are ideal if you would like to learn to skate after work as they are generally held at some convenient time in the early evening or during the weekend.

For the housewives and those of you who wish to skate alongside your toddlers, most ice rinks run mother-and-child classes. As with all groups, there will be a few professional coaches on hand to help you through any sticky moments.

These classes amount to a great combination of a coffee-morning atmosphere together with learning a new skill and keeping yourself fit at the same time.

The best way to gain a little insight into the workings of the sport is through these classes and apart from anything else it's good to take part in an activity that all the family can enjoy by either skating or spectating.

The rinks will have a system of awarding merit badges for progress in their classes and the national skating organizations also have various badges and proficiency tests available to encourage the advancing skater.

As you move on you may choose to learn one or all of the skating disciplines. These are divided into ice dancing, figure and free skating and pair skating.

Maria Usova and Alexander Zhulin, third in the 1991 World Ice Dance Championships

(There is a complete chapter on each of these topics later in the book and I haven't forgotten the aspiring ice hockey and speed skaters. Both of these topics are covered in Chapters 18 & 19.)

For the advancing skater, the ice rinks set aside times when the general public is not admitted and only the serious skaters can practise their moves. As you progress you will be able to take part in these sessions, in fact when you start to jump, spin and run through your own routine, this kind of scheduled practice time will be essential.

When you have worked your way through the classes you will have to find your own professional coach. All the rinks have some good coaches. There is usually a board up by the main office with photographs along with the names and teaching qualifications of the coaches.

It is a good idea to approach your favourite coach from the classes, and ask whether he or she has time to give you a fifteen-minute lesson. Your coach will be the best person to advise you on your skating career, when you have read this book; and if you are young, talented and highly motivated, it is always possible that you may become a champion. However, most people are content with becoming good recreational skaters as this is a realistic goal for any age group. Just about anybody can learn to skate a few simple ice dances and feel very accomplished in doing so. In fact, a recreational skater can have as much fun from skating a few simple steps as an advanced skater performing a great jump. This is the one sport that can be as exciting or relaxing as you wish. You, the skater, have some real control over your progress.

There are skaters I know of and one or two that I teach who are well into their seventies, ice dancing and going strong, so this is a sport for all ages, from tiny tots to the not so tiny tots!

Skating is a superb exercise for the whole body and can be a great aid to firming up many muscles that have become a little too relaxed and this exercise can be as gentle or as vigorous as you wish, dependent upon your individual requirements. Skating encourages people to stand up straight and hold their bodies well, thereby improving their posture. The sport can also be used to keep the elderly mobile.

Teaching one of my younger pupils, Dino, aged five

Another important psychological factor to consider is that skating gives everybody little goals to work for, along with the sense of achievement that each newly acquired move gives to the learner. Every new learning experience encourages another.

If you feel that physical participation in the sport is not for you, it is still possible to enjoy skating as a spectator. All you need is a little knowledge so that you can recognize the jumps, spins and dances along with knowing how the judges' marks are awarded. With this information you too, in your own way, can be part of the sport.

Costwise, ice skating compares favourably with a trip to the cinema or a cheap meal out, so it won't break the bank. Some ice rinks give reduced admission prices to the elderly and unemployed. Most ice rinks offer season tickets which can really cut the cost of your skating: the result being that the more often you skate, the lower the admission charge will work out.

In the United Kingdom, you can skate all year round. And as skating is an individual sport, you don't have to find a partner or organize a team to be able to enjoy yourself and practise at a time that suits you. You only have yourself to compete with – totally independent exercise! If you do want a partner, there is bound to be somebody who would like to skate with you.

Dealing with other areas of the sport, in the last few years there has been a great revival of interest in ice hockey. Although hockey has been played in Canada for over one hundred years, the new British rinks have been catching on in this area. With a little help from the North Americans, hockey is currently growing at an amazing rate. If this is your reason for skating, have a look at Chapter 19.

There is currently a good deal of support for speed skating with most rinks having clubs specifically for this purpose and ice time during which their members can practise.

Recent British successes have encouraged many new

people to get involved, so if you too would like to do the same, look at the appendix and contact the speed skating association for the address of your local club. For more basic information, start by looking at Chapter 21.

Ice rinks are generally open seven days a week during the mornings, afternoons and evenings, so have a look in the appendix at the back of this book for your nearest ice rink, and start skating.

Before we move on to the serious subject of modern ice skating in all its forms, we should take a look back in time and see where and how it all started.

Man has skated for thousands of years. He soon realized that gliding along the surface of a frozen river or lake was a rather good and effective way of moving about in winter and much easier and faster than walking.

However, as you can imagine, the equipment available in those days, due to the lack of technology, was extremely limited. I wonder how many modern skaters would be willing to skate on bones strapped to their feet. The lack of good equipment certainly held back the development of the sport and as a result skating remained restricted to a mode of winter travel for hundreds of years.

These early skaters (those poor people who used bones) propelled themselves along by sliding their feet and pushing forwards by way of sharp poles that they spiked into the ice to give some grip. Luckily, as time went by the technology and therefore equipment developed and later blades were made of wood, a material much easier to carve than bone. The first real breakthrough came in the eighteenth century. Even Queen Victoria and Prince Albert owned blades made for them by John Wilson, the famous Sheffield manufacturer. Ice-skating equipment was still rather primitive in those days. In fact, right through to the early part of this century, this equipment often consisted of a blade which was attached to a wooden fitting, which was then fastened to the skater's boots by leather straps. Other types of blade were fastened to the boots by strong metal clamps. Let's face it, skating on this kind of equipment must have been very difficult.

Speed skating became popular in the nineteenth century and racing events were organized in England in the Fen country.

Later in the century the first artificial ice rinks opened and it then became possible to skate all year round, even in places that didn't have cold weather as a matter of course.

Queens Ice Club in the 1950s The first mechanically refrigerated ice rink opened in 1876 in London, followed the same year by another in Manchester.

The next rinks of any real importance were Henglars, built on the site of the present London Palladium, and Princes Club in Knightsbridge, London. They were both rather exclusive and many of the world's top skaters were members. Henglars even held one of the early world championships. Both of these clubs had disappeared by the start of the First World War.

On the organizational side, the National Skating Association of Great Britain was formed in 1879, the United States Figure Skating Association in 1886, and the Canadian Figure Skating Association in 1888. When the National Skating Association was formed, two resolutions were passed by the members. Firstly it was decided to form a test structure with relevant medals to mark the appropriate level of achievement. Secondly there was an agreement to establish with other skating organizations a method of international competition. The formation of the International Skating Union was the eventual result of these efforts along with the World (and later the European) Championships.

On the technical side, some of the early skaters invented jumps that we still do today. Axel Paulsen and Ulrich Salchow both devised moves that are still performed by today's top free skaters, although in a rather more advanced form with three or even four turns in the air, compared to the singles of their inventors.

In the 1930s and '40s skating became popular through the great talent of skaters such as Sonja Henie, who organized ice shows and starred in films with ice-skating themes. This was one of the great periods of skating expansion and development, until the Second World War called a halt to the progress.

During the war years, there were no international events, but immediately afterwards the sport started to fly ahead.

There were great technical advances from the new generation of skaters, especially in the free skating.

Many of the multi-rotational jumps and complicated

Ulrich Salchow, the inventor of the Salchow jump spins seen today on our television screens were first developed and performed after the Second World War and we have the North Americans skaters to thank for this progress. They have since dominated many of the free-skating events.

Dancing on ice dates back to the late nineteenth century when waltzes on ice became popular, but the real developments came in England between the world wars. Most of the compulsory dances which are skated in the championships today were created by the top British ice dancers of the Thirties. Skating was a great social event at that time, especially at Queens Ice Club in Bayswater, London.

After the war ice dancing was included in the European and World Championships but it was not included in the Winter Olympic Games until 1976. This was partly due to the fact that it is usually the most popular audience event in the championships. Although it is an area currently dominated by the Soviet Union, British ice dancers come first in the total number of championship wins, Torvill and Dean being the most recent British, four times World Champions.

The compulsory or school figures formed a major part of all the championships until 1990 which was the last year of their inclusion, although they are still considered an essential part of the learning process. Looking to the future, television has caused great changes to take place within the sport. Some areas, such as compulsory figures, didn't make good viewing, so they had to go. This means that the future singles events will consist of free skating various lengths of programmes, with ever more difficult jumps. The free skaters of the future are surely going to be amazing as all the time spent on practising the compulsory figures can be put to developing their free skating skills.

The ice dancing remains much as it always has been, with the championships consisting of a couple of compulsory dances, an original-rhythm dance and a free dance of a specified length. In this area there have been some remarkable skaters, such as Torvill and Dean, whose contribution to the sport cannot be underestimated. They have tended to alter the course a little for the skaters that follow them.

The pair-skating events have been dominated by the

Soviet skaters, with only the occasional exceptional Canadian or American couple winning Worlds. As with all other aspects of the sport, the technical advances continue and each year some even more brilliant moves are performed to thrill the skating audiences and gain high marks from the judges.

In 1990 a new discipline was added. The International Skating Union recognized precision skating as a new competitive area within the sport. We have the Canadians to thank for developing and promoting precision. As team skating is involved, the number of participants in future events is bound to be high.

Ice hockey probably started in the North of England. It is believed to have been introduced to Canada by British soldiers in the nineteenth century. Some people believe that the original game took place in the 1860s in Kingston, Ontario, Canada. This may well be the case although there is a good deal of evidence to show that the game was played some years earlier in Halifax, Nova Scotia.

There is no doubt that the first organized game of ice hockey was played in 1875 in Montreal. McGill University had the first ice hockey club, in 1880 and naturally enough, Montreal became the early centre of the sport.

It now has an enormous following worldwide. The best known prize is that known as the Stanley Cup. This is a competition between the top North American teams. The competition was first organized in 1894 and the cup donated by the Governor General of the time, Lord Stanley of Preston.

In recent years there has been a revival of ice hockey in the United Kingdom and some of the teams are becoming highly competitive. It is worth recalling that the Olympic champions of 1936 were the British!

Returning to the speed skaters of the nineteenth century, it must be said that this branch of the sport is now very popular, having been helped by recent British success along with the general growth in the number of practice rinks. All things considered, the future looks very bright for the sport with many countries now able to produce competitors to represent them internationally in all areas of the sport.

2 *What To Wear*

Now that you have decided to take to the ice, you must consider which are the most suitable clothes to wear, bearing in mind the local skating conditions.

You may have already formed an impression as to the kind of outfits that skaters wear from your TV set. Although these clothes look impressive, they are impractical for the following reasons. These costumes will have been designed specifically to fulfil certain specialized requirements. They are usually intended to be descriptive of the character of the piece of music that the skater is using. As these outfits are worn only for competitions and shows, they are completely unable to withstand the rigours of practice conditions. Also, due to their specialized designs, they are rather expensive.

Skating clothes are required to perform several functions. Firstly, they must be practical. By this I mean that they must be hardy enough to withstand regular usage. Secondly, they should fit close to the body whilst allowing you the freedom to move comfortably. Thirdly, they should be attractively designed.

As you will be exercising hard on the ice, the clothes you wear must reflect the activity and give you the necessary physical freedom. You must feel comfortable in your clothing, as nothing can be worse than trying to skate in restrictive clothing. The next sections deal in detail with the most suitable clothing for your first skating session.

Clothes for your first trip

For your first trip to the ice rink you really must wear loose-fitting clothing. I would recommend tracksuit/jogging pants for both the guys and girls. These pants must be of the stretchy kind in order to allow the maximum body movement with the minimum resistance.

A young skater wearing ideal clothes for beginners

There are several additional factors to consider when choosing your jogging trousers. You must ensure that they are not very wide or long. This is because there is always the possibility that they could catch on the hooks positioned along the top part of the skating boot. They should also have at least one pocket, as you may need somewhere to store your keys or a little spending money.

As an alternative you could wear ski-suit trousers, although they tend to be a little hot indoors and don't allow quite the same freedom as the jogging pants.

In order to keep your upper body warm and yet allowing maximum freedom to move, wear a large loose fitting sweater or sweat shirt. However, if you feel this is not sufficient, you can always wear additional layers of clothing underneath. In fact several light layers of clothing are often more effective than a single heavy layer, along with the additional advantage to the skater of the ability to remove clothing after warming up and still have some more underneath.

Body protection must be given serious consideration, especially for the hands, the elbows and the knees. These exposed parts of the body can take frequent knocks in the event of falling.

Gloves are an essential part of the skater's equipment as they serve two important functions: keeping your hands warm and providing some good protection in the event of a fall. Sometimes there are areas of the ice surface which are not perfectly smooth and contact between your hands and these areas can be a little rough on the skin.

Young children under the age of five must wear some kind of head protection. This could be either a woollen hat or an ice-hockey helmet.

Take obvious precautions and ice skating will be safe as well as fun.

Clothes for skating outdoors

If you are going to skate outdoors, you must wear

clothes to suit the prevailing conditions. Once you have a good idea of the temperature in which you will be skating, you can decide what and how much to wear.

When the weather is really cold, you should wear a ski suit. Avoid wearing any clothing that will restrict your movement, so that means no long coats! You should also wear a woollen hat pulled down over your ears along with ski gloves. Keeping your head and hands warm is important, as you can lose much of your body heat through them.

Should the temperature be reasonably high, causing the surface of the ice to melt slightly, it may be advisable to take along a change of clothing in case your skating outfit gets a little damp.

Unsuitable clothing

Whatever else you wear, avoid wearing tight jeans. Although jeans are the standard casual dress, they do not lend themselves to ice skating for several reasons, the best being that they simply restrict your movement as denim has little give as a material; the result is an inability to bend your knees and glide without great difficulty.

Ice rinks are not as cold as you might think and even if they are, the exercise will warm you up very quickly. Bearing this fact in mind, avoid wearing heavy jackets unless they are short in length; knee length is the maximum acceptable and waist level is ideal.

If you need to wear a jacket, restrict yourself to the kind used for skiing as these are designed to allow maximum freedom – anything bulky tends to restrict your movement. The same point applies to coats of any description. There is a good simple question to ask yourself when considering the clothes that you should wear. Can I move easily in what I am wearing? If the answer is no, find something which allows you more freedom.

If you skate in high summer, resist the temptation to wear shorts and T-shirts as they give no protection at all. Ensure that your elbows and knees are covered at least until you are reasonably proficient.

Never take your personal stereo on to the ice. This is because you must give all your attention to what you are doing and listening to your own music will distract you. Don't carry bags of any description while skating.

Finally, avoid wearing any chunky jewellery, as this kind of thing can break into many pieces, causing great problems for all the other skaters.

Footware and protection

As your feet and lower legs will be taking most of the strain when you skate, be sure to give them adequate protection. Compared to just about any other kind of footware, skating boots are very strongly made. As a result, during a long skating session, they may well rub and cause problems, which can be avoided by taking a few simple precautions.

Firstly, always wear socks that come slightly above the level of the boot. Secondly, position a little foam rubber above and below the ankle bone, as this can be a potential sore spot. Should you feel that the foam rubber is in the way, you can always remove it and place it somewhere else. Take along additional pieces of foam rubber and plasters. They may be needed if the boots rub.

SUMMARY

For your first trip to the ice rink, ensure that you wear loose fitting clothing, preferably with a good deal of stretch. This applies to both the guys and the girls. Make sure that you have a pocket somewhere, to store your keys and a little money. Do not wear long jackets or coats. Ski jackets are the most suitable for skating. Wear gloves to protect your hands and long socks inside your skating boots.

The under fives must wear either a hockey helmet or a woollen hat. If you are wearing a scarf, do make sure that it is tucked well into your other clothing. Avoid carrying bags of any kind on the ice. Take some plasters and foam rubber to protect any sore spots that may appear during the skating session. Do not wear personal stereos as they reduce your attention level and may be broken if they fall on to the ice. Finally don't wear any chunky jewellery; if this breaks, it will take ages to pick up off the ice, and could be a hazard.

3 Your Boots and Skates

Ice skates consist of a strong boot with a metal blade attached to the sole. The boot is quite high, as it comes some way above the ankle bone and is fastened to the foot by long laces. Naturally enough ice-skating boots are designed to give the foot and lower leg maximum support.

In order to meet the stresses and strains to which they are subjected, the boots are made from several layers of leather reinforced with strong heel and instep supports. These supports ensure that the skater's foot is well supported, especially during difficult moves, turns and jumps.

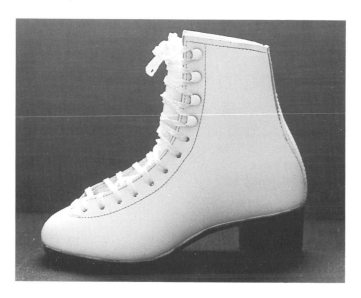

The blades, slightly longer than the soles of the skating boots, are made of hardened steel and fastened on by screws. At the front of each blade is the toe pick, which is a series of small sharp teeth used mostly to help the skater grip the ice surface when jumping or performing specialized footwork — not, as many people believe, for stopping!

Ice skates slide because friction between the blade and the ice surface causes the ice under the point of contact to melt briefly. The water formed under the skate acts as a lubricant causing it to slide. This water freezes again almost at once, leaving a mark or tracing on the ice surface. Wherever you skate you will be followed by your tracing.

The blades have two edges. The edge corresponding to the outside of your foot is called the outside edge and that corresponding to the inside of your foot, the inside edge. If you look at the diagram you will notice that the underneath of the blade, between the edges, is hollow in section. The blades are designed in this way in order to help you grip the ice at all times.

The extent of the hollow between the two edges, known as the 'grind', varies depending on the type of blade

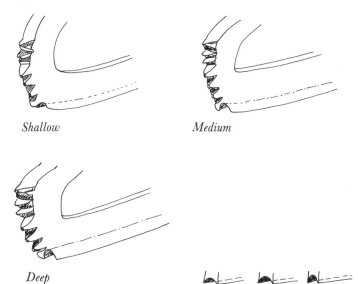

Shallow   Medium

Deep

You may think that balancing on a narrow blade is difficult enough, but most of the time the aim is to balance only on one edge, so that the blade is at an angle to the ice rather than completely vertical. Be assured that this feat is possible for most people.

Hiring your own boots

For your first few attempts it is wiser to hire skates at the rink rather than buy your own. It can be an expensive mistake to invest in equipment before you are sure you will skate regularly, and pointless to skate simply because you have bought the equipment.

All good ice rinks have a skate hire with a large selection of sizes, where you will be able to find some boots to fit your feet. They are usually made of leather though moulded plastic has become popular too and these are fine for your first few visits.

As with any pair of shoes, your skating boots must not be so small that they squash your feet. You should be able to move your toes around inside the boot without feeling that your heel can slip out. A good test for this consists of fastening the boots, then bending your knees and leaning forward, try to slide a finger down the boot and behind your heel. If there is enough room to do this the boots are too big and your heel may slip. Ask for the same size as your shoes, not half a size smaller as often recommended; and, above all, aim for comfort.

Before you put on your boots check two things. Firstly, ensure that all of the hooks are intact and secondly check the condition of the laces (not frayed). The laces must be correctly threaded all the way up the boot.

When fastening the boots take your time. Make sure you pull the laces securely through each eyelet so that there is minimal slack lower down the boot but enough to let you bend your ankles. They shouldn't be too tight towards the top because this can cause problems when bending your knees, resulting in rubbed skin and even blisters.

When you have fastened your boots stand up careful-ly and hold on to something (a wall will do nicely), as you may feel very wobbly. Put both feet together and try to bend your knees. Should your laces cut into you whilst you are bending, loosen the boots around the bend in the ankle and readjust them. If you feel your ankles are falling inwards or outwards then fasten the boots more tightly. If on readjusting the boots the ankles are still not held up straight, the boots may be faulty and you should try on another pair.

Should the boots press against you or cause any pain, pack the area with pads or foam rubber. The best way to protect sore spots is by making a bridge to take away the pressure. This is done by placing your foam above and below the trouble spot. Never put protective pad-ding on top of a sore spot, as this will only increase the pressure and the pain.

Finally, if you feel uncomfortable or are unhappy in any way change your boots.

Check your blades

You must make sure that the blades have fairly sharp edges. Should there be little or no edge you will have no grip on the ice. If in doubt, check with a professional or experienced skater on this point.

Ice skates should only move forwards or backwards and never sideways. If they skid sideways the blades are probably blunt. There is a very simple way to test the edges. Run the surface of your finger nail across the blade. If the blade is able to scrape some of the surface away from your nail, you have some edge. If not, ask for another pair of skates.

Your blades could also be too sharp, though this is unlikely. Over-sharpened blades tend to cut too deeply into the ice, causing the blade to travel slowly and turn with great difficulty.

SUMMARY

Ice skates consist of a strong leather or moulded plastic boot on to which a blade made of hardened steel is attached by screws.

The blades are several inches longer than the boots and have a series of sharp metal points, known as the toe picks at the front end. They are designed with two edges and a hollow/concave curve between them. This feature ensures maximum grip between the skate and the ice surface.

Skates glide because of their action on the ice surface. Pressure between the points of contact causes friction. As a result of this friction, the ice melts and the blade glides on the water which acts as a lubricant. The water freezes leaving a tracing in its place.

For your first trip to the rink, hire rather than buy equipment. Ensure that your feet are adequately protected, by way of foam/sponge/plasters. Always place padding around sore spots in such a way as to create a bridge which will lift any pressure away. Never place padding on top of sore spots, as this will aggravate the problem.

Check your equipment before use. Make sure that all the hooks are in place, that the laces are threaded through all the eyelets and that they are not frayed. Make sure that the blades are firmly attached to the boot. The skates should only slide forwards or backwards. If they slide sideways, take them back and ask for a pair with sharper edges. If you are unhappy with your equipment in any way, return it and ask for a replacement.

4 Buying Your Own Equipment

As you progress in your skating career, you will soon reach a point where rented skates start to hinder rather than help your progress. This is the time when you should seriously consider buying your own. (N.B. Although it would be correct to say that your immediate progress from day one would be faster in your own boots, this is a financial decision best left until you have positively decided to skate on a regular basis.)

The best places to buy ice-skating equipment are, naturally enough, the specialist suppliers, as they are most likely to have the greatest selection of goods along with the relevant expertise. (Some of the major U.K. and Canadian suppliers are listed in the appendix at the back of this book.)

Before setting out to buy your items of equipment, you must have a good idea as to the purpose for which you will be using them.

Ask yourself whether you plan to be a recreational, figure, hockey or speed skater, then go out and buy the most suitable equipment as outlined below.

Later chapters will explain in detail the different disciplines of skating, but briefly these are as follows:
Free skating jumping and spinning on ice
Ice dancing series of steps performed with a partner to a set musical tempo

Compulsory figures creating and tracing set geometrical patterns on the ice

Ice hockey playing hockey on ice

Speed skating the discipline that involves racing against either other skaters or a clock

Precision skating amounts to a group of skaters performing various steps and moves as a group to music

Recreational skating boots

Most people start out as recreational skaters and as such will tend to look for a product that is reasonably durable without being too expensive. Should you fit into this category, there are several options open to you, and quite a few manufacturers making good equipment. One of the best-known brands is Risport, which is a company with a good product range, from starter/ recreational stock right through to strong free-skating boots.

The recreational type of equipment generally amounts to what is known as a 'set': that is, skating boots with a blade already attached.

A basic set, suitable for beginners

Naturally enough, adults should consider buying a stronger make of boot than that bought for children as they will make rather heavier demands on the product. This often means buying a more specialized product. The next section deals with this area in greater detail.

More specialized skating boots

As you progress you would be well advised to consider buying more specialized equipment. Better boots and skates will help you progress more quickly whereas poorer quality goods tend to hold you back. This means buying your boots and blades separately and having them fitted to suit your needs. As a general rule it's worth paying the higher price for a good pair of boots as they will give you long-lasting service.

Most of the top boot makers offer a range of styles and strengths as well as all the popular sizes. Men's boots are usually black and ladies' white but some show skaters dye their boots flash colours for effect.

If you would like to be able to jump and spin, you will have to buy a very strong model of free-skating boot, as anything less will fall to pieces. The figure and dance boots tend to be a little less hard and robust, in accordance with the demands of the discipline. The strength and rigidity of the boot is generally reflected in the price, as stronger boots require more leather and extra internal supports, making them more difficult to work. Should you require something a little special — or, like me, have rather large feet — you would be well advised to read the next section.

Custom-made skating boots

The majority of the top championship skaters wear custom-made boots. This means boots that have been specifically designed and built to individual specifications. None of us has feet of exactly the same size so standard fittings can never be completely accurate. Hand-made boots overcome this problem and — surprisingly enough when one considers the amount of work involved — they do not cost that much more than the top off-the-shelf boots.

Generally, custom-made boots are fashioned in varying strengths, from firm, which are ideal for ice dancing, to extremely strong, which are ideal for the skaters working on their quadruple jumps. You can specify the colour, the type of lining you would like and whether or not you need any padding for sore spots.

In order to provide the manufacturer with all the necessary information and measurements for your feet, you will be sent a large form to complete in accordance with the instructions. When taking your measurements, you must wear the socks or tights that you use for skating. While you are being measured, make sure that your weight is equally distributed between your feet. When all the measurements have been taken, an outline of each foot must be drawn on the form.

This information will be sufficient to make you a superb pair of skating boots which should see years of service.

Breaking in your boots

The first time that you skate in your new boots, they will feel rather hard and difficult to bend. (Remember to protect your feet by way of packing above and below any potential trouble spots.)

As a general rule you would be well advised to keep your new boots quite loosely fastened, as a failure to do so may mean that you will have problems bending your ankles and knees. This will make your skating seem very difficult. At first your new boots will probably feel more difficult to skate in than hired boots until the leather creases in line with your ankle joints. This process of 'breaking in' will take about a dozen reasonably energetic skating sessions to complete.

N.B. If you are buying some skates for a young child (under 4 years of age), you could consider **runners**. Runners have two blades several inches apart and as a result are very stable and easy to stand up on. They are attached to the child's foot by plastic straps. These skates are not a good idea long term, and if you can find standard boots and blades small enough you would be well advised to do so.

Buying your own blades

When you buy your ice-skating boots you should ask the retailer to find out what size of blade should be fitted. This can be done by placing a blade on the boot with its front touching the front of the boot; the back of the sole plate must be located as close to the back edge of the heel as possible.

How to choose the size of blade

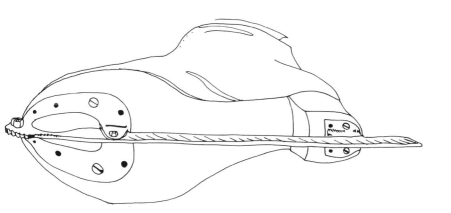

In order to acquire all the necessary knowledge of the equipment used in the sport, I visited John Wilson, the famous blade-maker. They have been in the business for centuries, so you can imagine how much experience they have.

There are quite a few processes involved in making blades, starting with a sheet of steel and ending up with a beautifully made piece of skating technology.

Before buying your blades, there are several important things for you to consider. Firstly, you must ask yourself for what purpose will they be required. By this I mean, will you need them for figures, free skating, or ice dancing.

Your local supplier or a professional skating coach will be the best person to advise. I would now like to tell you a little more about the various types of blades that you should consider — and all made by John Wilson.

Figure blades

These are blades specifically designed for skating compulsory figures. They have a rather shallow grind, in order to minimize the friction between the skate and the ice and therefore maximize the distance the skater can travel on each push. (This may involve travelling around two large circles with only one push to provide the speed.)

Free-skating blades

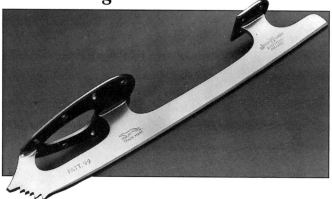

Free-skating blades are made to withstand all the stresses and strains put on them by the top free-skating champions. They have large toe rakes/picks and tend to have rather a deep grind to maximize grip between the skate and the ice.

Ice-dance blades

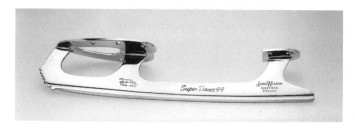

Ice-dance blades are quite different from the figure and free-skating blades. This is mainly due to their length. In order to avoid catching the partner's skates during intricate step sequences, the heel of the blade is short. They usually have quite a deep hollow grind.

Hockey and speed skates

You will notice that hockey skates do not have any picks on the front. The boots are much lighter and have lower heel and ankle supports than figure boots and they are popular with many young recreational skaters. But if you intend to learn any of the major moves and turns performed in free skating or ice dancing, you won't be able to do so! Some rinks have special sessions when you can use these skates and most have ice-hockey clubs and teams.

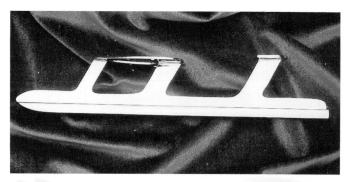

Speed skates are extremely long, flat and thin to enable the skater to travel quickly with the minimum of effort.

Fitting your blades

Your skates must be fitted by a specialist. Although it is important to centre the blades initially, many figure and dance skaters need the blades moved slightly to suit their individual requirements.

Your local rink should be able to provide this service.

Second-hand boots and skates

As a general rule, don't buy second-hand skating equipment. However, as children usually grow out of their boots rather than wear them out, if you can get hold of child's boots that are hardly used, you would be well advised to try them out.

Adults are usually much harder on their boots than children and second-hand equipment of this variety has generally seen better days.

Skating clothes

When you have bought your boots and skates, you should look at the various types of clothes available for the serious skater. The girls should buy skating skirts or dresses. These outfits are designed to allow the maximum amount of movement. They are usually made from stretchy lycra and are intended to fit you as closely as possible without cutting into your skin.

The guys generally wear stretchy trousers and these should be fastened by way of material or elastic straps to the underneath of the skating boots. This method may sound rather strange but it ensures a good body-line and helps the free leg and feet to look as neat as possible.

Some people prefer to wear 'all-in-one' outfits, which are fitted rather like one-piece ski suits. They tend to look best when worn by slim people.

If you have a partner, you should either wear the same colour outfit, or something that contrasts nicely. The best person to advise you in this area is your skating teacher or supplier.

N.B. If you plan to work through the various introductory lessons outlined in this book, you would be well advised to postpone the purchase of your outfit until you start lesson 6. However, many little girls try harder when wearing a new skating dress!

I would now like to add a few points regarding the type and style of clothes that you buy. The girls would be well advised to choose something dark in colour; black is ideal, as so many different outfits can be worn against it. It is probably the least restrictive shade to choose. Little children always look good in bright colours.

Completely white dresses should be avoided at all costs, for the following reasons. Firstly, unless you are extremely thin, you will not look good. White tends to make people look a little heavier than they are. Secondly, you couldn't get a more impractical shade, as it shows every mark. Thirdly, should you fall in water . . . well, I'll leave that one to your imagination. Lastly, you should ask yourself whether or not you want to look like a dying swan so early in your career.

For the guys, there are stretchy trousers, fastened to the boots, which can be obtained from the various equipment suppliers listed in the appendix. The main advantages of these trousers amount to allowing the skater great physical freedom, along with a good free leg line. If your trousers are not tied to your boots, it is rather difficult for others to notice whether or not your free leg is completely straight.

Bystanders may get the impression that you are less competent than you really are, if you fail to wear clothes that are designed for skating.

For the upper body, a sweater or sweat shirt remains the most suitable clothing, and you can wear almost any kind of shirt underneath.

A suitable boy's skating outfit: tied down trousers and a sweatshirt

Caring for your equipment

Your boots and blades are expensive, so it makes sense to look after them.

Clean your boots frequently with the relevant colour renovating polish, which is supplied at most ice rinks/ shoe stores.

Make sure you dry and polish your blades after each skating session or they will become rusty. That will make your skating difficult and shorten their life!

It's a good idea to buy a pair of rubber or plastic skate guards — especially if your local ice rink has areas which are not covered by rubber matting. Guards will protect your blades when you walk over concrete or wood. Never store your skates with the guards still in place, as this can encourage rusting.

Every time you finish skating, check that your blades are still tightly fastened to your boots, as the screws will tend to loosen with time and wear.

Periodically, after approximately 20–30 hours of skating, you should have your blades sharpened (reground). This figure for regrinding should only be taken as a guide and not an absolute, as some people like their skates to be sharper than others.

The blade manufacturers or your local agent will offer this service.

SUMMARY

After you have been skating for a while, you should buy your own equipment. There is a list of suppliers in the appendix at the back of this book.

You must decide whether or not to buy recreational or specialized goods. Adults generally require more strongly made boots than children. For very young children, who are unable to find skates small enough, there are runners.

As a general rule, don't buy second-hand equipment.

If you are a recreational skater, that is someone who only wishes to skate occasionally, forwards and backwards, your local supplier or ice rink will be able to advise you of their product range.

If you want to be able to use the boots for figures, free skating and ice dancing, you should buy a specialized product. You can order your boots in varying strengths. For free skating, you will need stronger boots than for ice dancing. It is usual to buy your boots and blades separately. You should buy the blades that are most suited to the area in which you plan to specialize.

For hockey and speed equipment, you should contact one of the suppliers named in the back of this book, as they will have experts on hand to advise you.

Great care must be taken with your equipment. Dry the blades and soles of your boots after every session. Wear guards when walking to and from the ice surface. Never store blades with the guards in place. Clean and restore the leather with the relevant renovating polish.

After every session, check your skates for tightness and sharpness.

5 *Safety On Ice*

Ice skating is about having good, safe fun. In order to be able to do so, every skater must be aware of the basic safety rules that apply on every ice rink. Before stepping out on to the ice, make sure that your body is adequately protected. Any children under five must wear either a woollen hat or a hockey helmet and everybody should have their knees and elbows covered. Even in the summer, avoid wearing shorts and T-shirts, that leave your knees and elbows unprotected.

Ice rinks usually have a list of rules in a prominent position, close to the ice surface. Most of these rules amount to having consideration for other skaters and I shall cover the most important in the following section, but first of all, a few words about how the ice surface is policed.

All good ice rinks have stewards on duty during public sessions. This is to ensure safety, good order and happy skating according to the rules. Follow their instructions at all times and if they ask you to keep a particular area clear, there will be a good reason for this, and you must do as they say.

In order to have some control over the flow of skaters around the ice surface, it is necessary for everybody to skate in the same direction. This direction is usually anticlockwise, but on some rinks it is the norm to alternate the direction from time to time. Bearing this information in mind, before you start, watch the other skaters for a while and check out the direction in which

A busy skating rink, showing all skaters moving in the same direction

they are skating and do the same. Before stepping on to the ice, check that the edges of your skates are clear of any gum or paper. To ensure this is so, clean your blades with a paper tissue.

Always look where you are going. This may seem an obvious thing to say, but the majority of new skaters are so involved in what they are doing that they simply don't pay attention to other people. So before you start any move check all around and make sure that you will be able fit your move in the space and time available, considering the relative positions and speed of the other skaters using the rink.

Before changing your own position on the rink, check that you are not becoming a hazard in the process. At first, if you are aware of another skater coming near you, it may be a good idea to move out of the way, rather than make them move for you. If you cannot move quickly enough, make this fact clear. As a general rule, let faster and better skaters have priority.

As you progress and begin to practise backward skating, be aware of the people near you, especially small children, as they are more difficult to spot.

N.B. Small children and the occasional adult have a tendency to skate directly from the move that they have just completed, straight to their friends or parents. Be aware of this possibility.

There is also a tendency for many learners to look straight ahead when practising backwards. This is equivalent to reversing your car when looking straight ahead, so make sure you look where you are going, not where you have come from!

Any paper handkerchiefs, keys or old chocolate wrapping papers that you may have in your pockets, must stay there. If you pull anything out of your pockets, such as a paper tissue, make sure that none of the previously mentioned articles, or any other for that matter, fall on to the ice. It they do, they will almost certainly become hazardous to other skaters. It's a good idea to check the surface of the rink for any foreign substances of this type, and if you find anything other than ice, please pick it up and place it into the garbage container.

Generally, the centre of the rink is kept free for either learners having lessons or more advanced skaters practising their moves. When you start, you do not need to go into the middle and if you do, you may well be asked to keep closer to the sides.

Keep your own maximum speed down to the same level as the rest of the skaters and make sure that you are able to stop at that speed. If you can't, slow down a little. Reasonable speed must be maintained.

Never take any drinks or food on to or near to the ice surface. If they spill they can easily become a problem. This applies to the smokers too. Never on the ice please.

Moving on to those of you who possess inquisitive minds, althought it may be tempting to test the depth of the ice surface using your picks, avoid this pastime as it causes a great deal of bad feeling and damage to the ice. If you need to know the depth, I can tell you that it will be about 2 in. or 5 cm. Finally, although the act of throwing ice and snow may appear to be harmless, avoid doing so, as this only causes aggravation.

SUMMARY

Before stepping on to the ice make sure that you wear

adequate protection. Be sure that hands, knees and elbows are covered. Children under five must wear a protective hat. Check the edges of your skates before stepping on to the ice.

Read the list of rules posted near the ice surface. Skate in the same direction as everybody else, usually anticlockwise. Obey the ice stewards. Keep the centre clear for people taking lessons and those practising specialized moves.

Always look where you are going, especially when changing your relative position on the rink.

Give priority to faster and more advanced skaters. Keep your own speed down to the average on the rink, or the speed at which you can stop safely, whichever is the lower.

When skating backwards, look behind you. Watch out for small children.

Never take any food or drink on to or near the ice, as any spillage can be hazardous to others. No smoking whilst skating. If you remove any article from your pockets, be sure that nothing falls on to the ice. Check the ice surface for any foreign objects and if you find any, please put them in the garbage container.

Never kick the ice surface with your picks and avoid throwing snowballs.

6 *Lesson One*

Now that you have turned to this section of the book, you may well have taken the decision to venture forth on to the ice.

I hope you will have read the earlier chapters, or at least the summaries, as they will fill any major gaps in your knowledge. If you haven't managed this to date, please do so before going on to the ice.

As this will probably be your first trip to an ice rink, I will try and give you some ideas as to what to expect and give a little insight into the workings of the ice rink.

After you have paid your admission and skate-hire charge, you will have to find the skate hire and exchange the relevant ticket, along with your shoes, for some suitable skates. It is a normal practice for the skate hire to keep your shoes as security for the skates. This also saves you the trouble of finding a locker in which to store them.

When you get your skates, check the general condition. Don't expect to get a new pair, but at the same time make sure that they look in reasonable shape. All the hooks should be in place. Check the placement, length and condition of the laces, as they mustn't be too short or frayed. If the skates seem reasonable try them on and fasten the laces securely, then stand up and place your feet together. If the skates feel quite comfortable and hold your ankles up straight they are probably good enough. Now bend your knees and, if the boots resist you a great deal, loosen them a little but if they don't resist you at all, tighten them up and re-test. If you still have problems exchange and re-test.

Before moving out of the skate hire, check that the blades are tightly fastened to your boots. If they are loose, there is usually a rattling sound when you walk. If you are wearing your own equipment, remove any skate guards. Skating with plastic covers on your blades is not recommended!

You are now ready to take your first steps. Walk carefully to the ice pad, making sure that you lift your feet on every step. Should you fail to do so, the picks can catch in the rubber matting and you may well end up skating along sooner than you had planned.

As you approach the ice, you will see that it is surrounded by a wooden or plastic barrier otherwise known as the boards which is about one metre in height. This is an extremely useful device as it can be used for support when stepping on and off the rink and when you just want to have a rest.

In the next section I am going to fill in a few relevant details relating to the workings of an ice rink.

The ice pad and how ice is made and resurfaced

The ice pad consists of a concrete area of about 60 metres in length and between 26 and 30 metres in width, built on top of strong foundations.

On the mechanical side, plastic pipes containing appropriate chemicals run through the concrete quite close to the surface. These chemicals are continually pumped through the pipes, causing the surrounding temperature to drop. (When the ice is laid initially, fine layers of water are sprayed on to the concrete and in a matter of a few days, the ice becomes thick enough to skate on.)

The ice surface is cleaned every few hours or so by a machine which is rather like a gigantic vacuum cleaner. This machine is often a Zamboni, which is probably the best known ice-resurfacing machine. During this cleaning operation the surface of the ice is scraped clear and a layer of warm water is spread over the surface, which then freezes, leaving a smooth sheet ideal for skating. If you haven't been to an ice rink before, you will find this process fascinating and it only takes somewhere around fifteen minutes. Great fun to watch!

The ice is resurfaced before skating in some rinks and afterwards in others.

CROSS SECTION OF AN ICE RINK

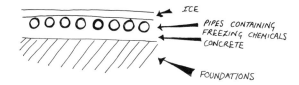

On to the ice!

Make your way towards one of the openings in the barrier and, while holding on to the side, make sure that the edges of your blades are clear of any contaminations such as gum or paper that you may have caught on the way to the ice surface. (Note that skaters usually travel around the ice surface in an anticlockwise direction. Just to be sure, check the direction and do likewise.)

At this point, I want to mention a couple of important words which will occur frequently throughout the learning sections. The first is 'skating leg' and the second is 'free leg'. The skating leg is the one on which you are standing and the free leg is that which is raised off the ice.

You are now ready for your big moment!

Keep hold of the barrier with your right hand and gently lift your left foot down on to the ice surface. (The ice pad is usually about six inches lower than the surrounding area.)

Now lift the right foot on to the ice, placing it next to the left. (You may prefer to follow these instructions using the other foot.) You must now think a little about your skating position. Contrary to popular belief, you should hold your body up rather straight, with your head, shoulders, hips and feet in line with your skating foot (the one on which you are standing). The shoulders must be relaxed, the skating knee slightly bent. Hold your arms out with your hands at about waist level. Now let's try some forward skating.

Stand with both feet together and bend your knees.

Hold your left arm out to the side, at about waist level; the right hand should still be holding on to the barrier.

Stage 1: forward skating

Your arms will help you to balance, so remember to keep them out to the side in the early stages. Now let's go for it! You are ready for **Stage 1: forward skating**. Take a deep breath and place one foot in front of the other, repeat the move with the other foot, and walk along the ice. This is the best way to start. Much of your skating progress is dependent upon your confidence and belief in your own ability, so be really positive.

Make sure that you keep your feet close together in between steps. If you feel at all nervous when your skate slides, bend the knee you're standing on and this will increase your level of control and balance.

Now move a couple of feet away from the barrier and repeat the move. Travel around the rink a few times using this method in order to build up your balance and confidence.

After a while, you will feel your skates gliding a little; this is fine, but make sure you keep the feet close together in between every step. Keeping the feet together ensures that your weight stays over your skates so that you remain balanced.

This is the right time for you to try some **forward sculling**.

(At this point, you should be thinking a great deal about bending the knee you are standing on, in fact as you read on you will notice that I mention bent knees a great deal.)

Stage 2: forward sculling

Now for some forward sculling. Forward sculling is a great way to move yourself along in the early stages of your skating, as you can feel your skates glide under you in a secure way. (This is mainly because you have both feet on the ice.) Children seem to love this move, falling over in the process if they can!

Stand with your feet together. Bend your knees and turn your toes outwards at the same time as keeping the heels together. The end result of this should be the feet forming a letter V shape. Slide both feet apart, by pushing the toes outwards, pressing on the insides of the feet at the same time. When the skates are a couple of feet apart, turn the toes inwards, straighten the knees slightly and draw the skates back together. Repeat.

The dip

At this point it's a good idea to try and skate along bending your knees as low as possible, so that you can touch the underneath of your skating boots.

Make sure that you keep your feet together!

This is a great move for building your confidence along with exercising and strengthening your knees. Children usually love this move as they can fall over at the end and practise getting up as described towards the end of this chapter.

Stage 3: forward gliding

The previously mentioned techniques are ideal as an introduction and amount to the first two stages in learning how to move across the ice. If you feel reasonably confident using these techniques you are ready to learn a more advanced method (stage 3).

Place your feet in a letter L position with the heels together and the right foot pointing forward, as shown in the diagram, below, and bend your knees.

The basic position ready to push

Slide your right foot a couple of feet away from you and then lift your left foot up alongside it, returning your feet to the letter L position, this time with the left foot pointing forward. Repeat the move with the left foot, sliding it away and then lifting the right foot up to it.

Start by taking small slides, and as you become more confident, increase the size of the step. It's a good idea to think of bending your knees at the start of each move and straightening them a little as you bring the feet back together. Make sure that you keep the knee you are standing on relaxed during each slide.

(If you are not taking lessons from a professional coach watch how experienced skaters move and take some feedback from their progress.)

The next section covers **backward skating**. Even on your first visit you may well be able to have a go, so I would recommend reading the section if for no other reason than to understand what it is all about and to realize why we need to skate backwards at all.

Stage 1: Backwards

For many people the idea of skating backwards is seen as a great skill, in fact many people who take skating lessons ask the question, 'Is it difficult to skate backwards?' followed by, 'Can you show me?' In reality, most people are able to learn a little of the required technique soon after they have gained their forward balance and, as a rule, I teach it to pupils in their first lesson.

A great deal of backward skating is required whichever discipline(s) of the sport you decide to undertake. In ice dancing both parties perform steps whilst skating backwards, although there is a tendency for the girl to do more of this than the boy. In free and pair skating, many of the moves are performed from backwards, as are nearly all jumps and spins. Bearing these facts in mind, the importance of backward skating cannot be underrated and anyway it's great fun.

The simplest way to move backwards is by way of **sculling** and the next section will cover this in some detail.

Backwards sculling

Stand with your feet together. Bend your knees and turn the toes inwards so that they are touching and forming an inverted letter V (fig.1). Press on the insides

Backward sculling

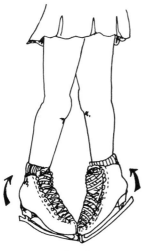

fig. 1

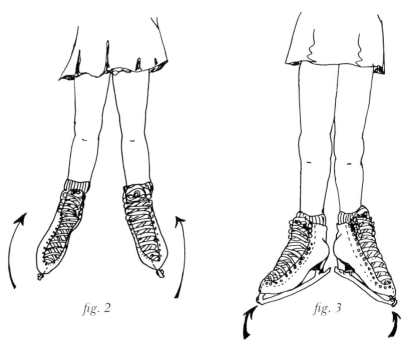

fig. 2 *fig. 3*

Backward of your feet and push the heels outwards. Make sure
sculling that both feet are moving apart at the same time and
with the same speed (fig.2). When your feet are about
18−24in. apart straighten up the knees and pull the
heels together. Bend the knees, turn the toes in and
repeat (fig.3).

It would be a good idea to practise this method of
backward skating for some time before moving on to the
more advanced techniques that are covered in later
chapters. However, there is one move that is even more
important than learning to skate backwards and that is
how to stop!

Stopping

This section deals with two of the easiest ways used for
stopping. As you will appreciate, the ability to stop is
one that must be acquired as soon as possible after
starting to skate, and until that time arrives, you should
stay close to the barrier (you can always crash into it).
The following section deals with the **T-stop**, which

most people will be able to put into practice on their first skating trip. The second stop mentioned, the **snow plough**, is slightly more difficult and may need a little more practice. Follow the instructions for each and try them both out as it is a good idea to perfect both methods.

T-stop

The T-stop involves skating on whichever leg is your stronger and then turning your back foot (the free foot) at 90 degrees to the skating foot. (N.B. The skating foot is the one on which you are standing.) Drag the free foot gently along the ice behind you using it as a brake and without putting much weight on it. The feet should form a letter T pattern during the move. If this move is causing great problems check two important points: firstly, make sure that your free foot is turned out sufficiently, and secondly that you are not putting too much weight on that foot when placing it down on the ice.

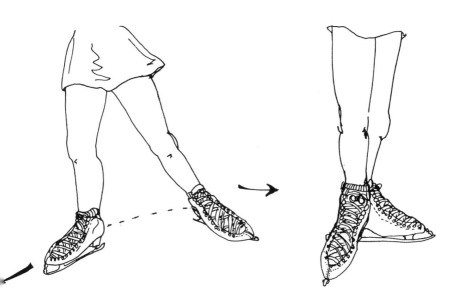

Snow plough

Work up some speed then glide along with your feet about 18in. apart. Bend both knees slightly and then while turning your toes inwards, push the feet apart, forwards and outwards, scraping the top of the ice surface with the inner edges of your blades as you do so. You should come to a stop after several feet of forward progress. This stop is called the snow plough because that's what it looks like!

As with the T-stop, practise this move until you feel confident of your ability to stop in an emergency.

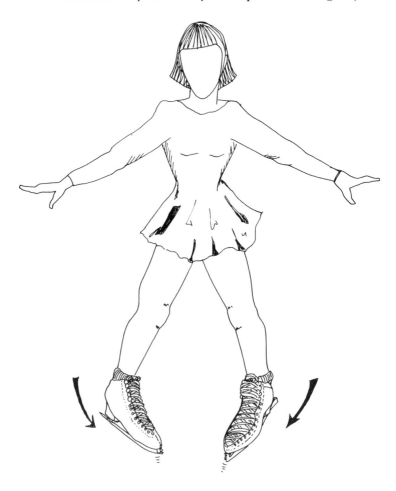

The next section deals with an inevitable topic, that of **how to get back on to your feet after a fall**. Falling is part of skating and should this occur, you will simply slide along, so, if you feel that this is about to happen, try to relax your body.

It is sometimes possible to save yourself from falling by bending your knees; however on your first visit it would be good practice for you to fall over and then try to get up again. (In the event of a fall, try to keep your hands out of the way.)

At first getting up will present a few problems and the next section will give you a proven survival technique, so read it through and practise it on dry land.

How to get up after a fall

Starting from a sitting position, roll over on to your stronger side and move to a kneeling position, placing your hands on the ice to hold you steady. Place your stronger foot on the ice and straighten that knee and push yourself up. As you progress you will find other, possibly unique ways of achieving the same result.

SUMMARY

Before reading this summary, you would be well advised to glance back at the earlier chapters, or at least the summaries.

After paying your admission and skate-hire charges, you will find the skate hire. Your shoes will be kept as security for the hire skates. Check the condition of the skates, making sure that all the hooks are in place. The laces should be of sufficient length and in reasonable condition. If the blades are loose they will rattle and you should exchange them. The boots should give sufficient support to hold your ankles and lower legs vertically, whilst allowing your knees to bend.

When walking to the ice pad, lift your feet, or they will catch in the rubber matting and you will start skating sooner than you had planned.

The ice surface is surrounded by a wooden/plastic

barrier (the boards), which is ideal to hold on to during critical moments. The ice is resurfaced by a kind of enormous vacuum cleaner, which removes all the debris on the surface and replaces it with a layer of water. When the resurfacer has finished, step on to the ice, making sure that your head is in line with your shoulders, hips and feet. The skating leg/knee is the one on which you are standing. The free leg/knee is that which is raised off the ice.

The skating knee should be slightly bent, and the arms held out to give balance. Stage 1: Start by walking on the ice. Always take small steps, keeping the feet close together. If necessary hold on to the barrier with one hand. Stage 2: Forward Sculling. Stand with both feet on the ice in a letter V position with your heels together. Bend both knees and push the feet apart. Turn the toes inwards and draw the feet together. Stage 3: Forward Gliding. Stand with your feet in a letter L position and slide on to the right foot, bring the feet together and repeat with the other foot leading. Increase the size of glide as your confidence increases. Make sure that you bend the skating knee during the glide.

Backward skating is an essential part of all aspects of the sport. Backward sculling is the simplest way to start off. Stand with your feet together and toes turned in to form an inverted letter V. Bend both knees and push the feet apart at the same time and with the same speed. When they are 18in. apart, turn the heels inwards and draw the feet back together. Turn the toes inwards and repeat.

Stopping involves using either the T-stop or the snow plough. 1: T-stop. Stand on your stronger leg and turn out your free foot at right angles to the skating foot. Gently drag the free foot along the ice until you stop. Your feet should form a letter T in the process.

2: snow plough. Work up some speed and glide along with the feet about 18in. apart, running parallel. Bend both knees and turn the toes inwards. Push the feet apart, forwards and outwards, rather like a snow plough.

Getting up after a fall involves attaining a kneeling position, using your hands to hold yourself steady. Place the stronger foot on the ice and use it to push yourself up.

7 Lesson Two

Your second visit will hold far fewer surprises than your first. You will know exactly what to expect as the system operating in your rink will no longer be a mystery.

You may have decided to buy your own boots and skates and if this is the case, I hope that you will have borne in mind the information contained in Chapter 4. If you are still using hired skates, you will have become wiser and no doubt will be able to find a better pair preferably with reasonably sharp edges, more quickly than you did on your first visit. If you find a pair that you really like, it may be a good idea to note the relevant number that you should find printed somewhere on the sole and make sure that you get that pair each time.

Talking about your outside and inside edges is one of the major topics covered in this chapter along with some more advanced moves to keep you busy.

I feel sure that by now you will have reached your own conclusions as to which are the most suitable clothes for you personally to wear whilst skating.

The chances are that you will have gained your balance, but if you are still not sure of your abilities, repeat the contents of the last chapter for this skating session. Moving on, I am now going to talk a little more about edges.

Your edges

It is absolutely essential for all skaters to know a little

about the edges of their skates and the uses for which they are intended.

As you will know from Chapter 3, the blade has two edges, the outside and the inside and these edges correspond to the outside and inside of the skater's foot. To be able to advance to the next stage in your skating career, some basic information regarding edges is needed.

When gliding along either forwards or backwards, you are generally on one edge or the other. A reasonably advanced skater will tend to glide towards the outside edge, whereas the absolute beginner will most probably be gliding along more on the inside than the outside, or perhaps on both at the same time. For a skater to be travelling on the outside edge, there is a physical requirement that the skating foot is slightly tilted towards the outside. This is to maximize the contact of that edge with the ice and the skater causes this to happen by leaning towards the outside edge required, either on the left or the right foot, forwards or backwards.

The result of this action is a glide on a curve. Exactly the same conditions apply when skating any of the inside edges, forwards or backwards. This is caused by the body lean of the skater.

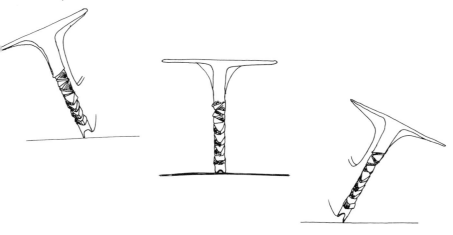

When a skater pushes, he will generally be applying pressure from the inside edge of the pushing foot. This naturally enough means that he will be pressing on the inside edge of the foot that he is standing on.

Look at the diagram above and see how the skate looks in cross section. You can see both the outside and the inside edges with the hollow in between them.

If a skater stands vertically, at right angles to the ice pad, both edges will be in contact with the ice and if he glides forward holding this position he should be travelling in a straight line. This contact is known as a 'flat' or 'double line'.

For the purposes of your second visit this is all the information on edges that you will require.

Stage 4: forward skating or forward stroking

This is the principal method used for skating forward at all levels and the following section covers the necessary technique in detail.

Stand with your feet together and bend both knees. Place your heels together with the feet forming a right angle.

Forward skating
Press on the inside edge of the pushing foot and slide on to the front foot.

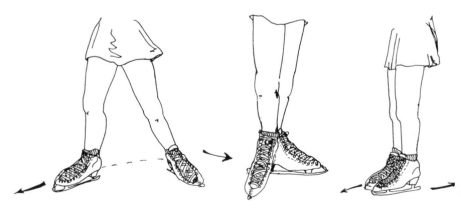

On the end of the slide, stretch the pushing foot back and hold it there for a couple of seconds. The extended free leg should be straight with the free foot turned out as closely as possible to right angles to the skating foot.

Bring the feet back together and repeat the move with the other foot. This is the most effective technique for skating forwards and should you have any great difficulties, watch out for other, more advanced skaters and model your stroking on them.

N.B The accuracy of your posture and stance is vital to your balance and progress. Your arms should be held out to the side with your hands at about waist level. Make sure that your shoulders are at right angles to the skating foot, or square to the direction in which you are moving.

Practise this move until you feel reasonably confident, as this is the one on which the basis of your forward skating depends. All these accomplishments will boost your self confidence and spur you on to achieve further skills of which the next one to cover is **Stage 2: backwards**.

Stage 2: backwards

In the last chapter, I introduced backwards skating by the technique of sculling. This enabled the new skater to have the security of both feet while moving backwards. Having gained the necessary confidence, it is time to move on to **Stage 2: backwards**.

This involves pushing and then transferring the body weight from one foot to the other and in doing so, provides a gentle and safe introduction to backwards skating on one foot.

In order to accomplish this move, stand with your feet together, with the toes turned inwards to form an inverted letter V. As usual the knees must be bent. Try to keep your head, hips and feet in line and hold the arms out with the hands at or below waist level.

Keeping both knees bent, press on the insides of your feet and push the heels outwards. Remember that, as with backwards sculling both feet must travel apart at the same time and with the same speed. When the feet are approximately eighteen inches apart, transfer the weight from one foot to the other by placing the relevant foot next to the one still on the ice. Repeat the moves mentioned above, transferring the weight to the other side.

N.B. Do make sure that you are looking where you are going so as to ensure that you do not become a hazard to yourself or to other ice users. Turn around and look behind you after every couple of pushes.

By now you will be aware that certain areas of the ice pad are used for different activities. There are often people taking lessons in the centre and sometimes others practising nearby. In some rinks you will notice that the professional coaches seem to keep a specific area clear of traffic so that their students can perform their moves.

You may well have heard the ice stewards telling skaters to keep out of the centre and close to the sides, not forgetting to skate in one direction only.

Practise the two methods of stopping as described in the last chapter so that you are able to react effectively to different ice traffic conditions.

When you wish to turn corners use the simple technique of turning your shoulders towards the direction to which you wish to move. Turning your head will have an additional effect as you can easily imagine that wherever your head goes you will have to go too.

Now that you are gaining additional skills make sure that you practise them at some distance from the barriers. It is inevitable that as you progress in your skating career the barrier can become more of a hazard than a friend. Therefore practise your moves within the spatial limits of the ice pad, away from the sides.

SUMMARY

This chapter assumes that you have already visited an

ice rink. By now you have learned the system operating in your local rink. You will have gained much relevant knowledge pertaining to the equipment required along with a basic skating technique.

If you feel in any way unsure of the moves attempted on your first visit, spend your second and if necessary the third visit repeating them. Building your self confidence is essential to your skating progress.

Ice skates have two edges, the outside and the inside, which correspond to the outside and inside of your feet. On your second visit some knowledge of edges is essential.

Generally when skating forwards, people glide on their outside edges. The inside edges are most often used to grip the ice whilst pushing. Good pushing usually involves applying pressure to the ice via the inside of the pushing foot.

If you are gliding on a particular foot and cause the skate to tilt towards the outside edge by leaning your body, the skate will tend to curve towards that direction. If you lean towards the inside edge the skate will tend to curve towards that direction. If both edges are on the ice at the same time, this is known as a 'flat'.

Stage 4: forward stroking is the most important forward push in skating. To be able to do this, stand with your feet placed at right angles, the heels touching and the knees bent.

Slide the skating foot forwards, stretching the free foot behind you. The free leg should be turned out at right angles to it. The free leg must remain stretched for a couple of seconds, although the length of time can vary according to the effect desired and the move being performed.

Stage 2: backwards is a good way of learning to skate backwards, transferring your body weight from one side to the other. Stand with the feet together, form your feet into an inverted V with your toes touching and bend both knees. Pressing on the insides of your feet, slide both feet apart at the same time and with the same speed. When the feet are approximately eighteen inches apart, lift one foot across and place it against the side of the other one. Repeat with the other side.

8 *Lesson Three*

By now I hope that you are reasonably pleased with your progress and gaining confidence with every step.

At this time, I would like to point out to you the importance of warming up your body before going on the ice.

Your body will work much better if your skating muscles have been stretched and worked a little before any hard physical exercise is demanded of them. The best way of warming up is by way of gentle exercise.

In a cold ice rink, you can reduce the likelihood of muscle strain if you follow the instructions given below.

Stand with your feet together, holding on to either the back of a chair or some similar object. Keeping your back straight, your feet together and your head up, bend your knees until the backs of your thighs touch the backs of your lower legs. Straighten up your knees until they return to a standing position and repeat the exercise, perhaps ten times, building up to about twenty over a period of a few skating sessions.

Many other skating exercises are useful too, such as cycling and specifically designed weight lifting and training programmes.

If the rink tends to be rather cold, wear several light layers of clothing, so that as your body warms up, you will be able to remove the occasional sweater and keep your body temperature comfortable.

By now, you should be able to move around the ice without too many problems as well as stop in an emergency and maybe even skate a little backwards too. If you are having problems, continue to practise the moves covered on the first and second visits; only when you feel confident with these should you move on to the next stage.

At this stage, many of you will have bought your own boots and skates. As your new boots are likely to be considerably stronger and less flexible than your hire boots, you would be well advised to start out with the laces rather loosely fastened.

You can try them out and should you find the need to tighten them up a little, you can easily do so.

Make sure that your blades have been correctly positioned. Although there is no absolutely perfect spot to which the blades should be fastened, there is a general rule applicable to all blades and this amounts to the blades being fitted in a straight line and as centrally as possible. (Please note that the seam which runs down the front and back of the boot can be used as a generally accurate guide line.)

As a double check, hold the boot up at eye level, then placing the blade against it, check that it is positioned in the middle of both the sole and the heel.

A good dealer will have fitted your boots and blades as described above, but with the screws attached to the two slot holes in each of the sole and heel plates. This enables the skater to try out the new equipment and should there be any serious problems, the positioning of the blade can be altered to meet individual requirements.

N.B. It is important to note that the blades should never be attached to the sole using all of the available screw holes, until the skater has decided upon the ideal position. To find this out there is a simple test which can be carried out in the following manner:

Stand with your feet together and use the Stage 4: forward stroke, as described in the last chapter, then push and glide on to the right foot. Be certain that you are travelling in a straight line with your skating foot held vertically and the free leg held out in line with your skating foot. To ensure a straight line it is a good idea to skate towards the barrier.

While gliding along, judge whether or not your skate is trying to pull you towards one direction or the other. This would feel as if the skate were trying to turn.

If the skate is not pulling you in either direction, it has been correctly fitted, but if you are being pulled towards either the inside or outside edge, a slight adjustment to the position may be necessary.

Should the skate pull to the inside it may be necessary to move the skate slightly to the outside of the boot. If it pulls to the outside perhaps the skate should be moved in slightly. Other possibilities could be along the lines that the blade has not been put on straight or the blade requires the placement of packing between itself and boot to fill in any gaps between the two. This can be caused by the fact that the soles of skating boots are often slightly curved rather than completely flat.

Whatever else you do, consult an expert before making any radical changes to the blade placements and only when the exact position has been achieved should you fit the remaining screws.

N.B. After every subsequent visit to the ice rink, check that your blades are still firmly attached to your boots, as they will tend to work loose. Bearing this in mind, many skaters carry a screwdriver in their skate bags.

Now apply the same test to the left foot and adjust or leave the skate accordingly. When the exact position has been achieved, make sure that the skate is securely fastened and fit the remaining screws.

Tighten the screws until the blade is held firmly against the boot, but be sure to avoid over tightening as this can cause the screw to rip out the leather that is holding it in place.

Now to continue with the third visit.

Before stepping on to the ice, warm up your body by working through the exercises described at the start of this chapter; and, keeping along the same lines, you would be well advised to use the first ten minutes of the skating session revising the moves learned on your previous visits. This means practising your forwards and backwards skating along with a few T- and snow plough stops. Then you will be ready to try **Stage 5: forwards or forward glides** and the next section deals with the relevant details.

Stage 5: forwards or forward glides

Stand with your feet together and bend both knees. Using the technique described in the last chapter under **Stage 4: forward skating or forward stroking**, take three pushes, gliding on to the right foot first. After you have completed the third push, stand on a bent knee travelling in a straight line with both edges in contact with the ice.

Forward glide

During the glide, you must hold your body in such a way as to ensure that your head, shoulders, hips and skating foot are in line with each other. Repeat this procedure, gliding on to the left foot first. These forward glides are great fun to practise and are a good gauge of your progress. If you can control your direction sufficiently well to be able to hold the position for several seconds, you are coming along very well. If you can't quite make it, don't be downhearted, as this is par for the ice-skating course.

At this stage there is a great danger of a major fault developing. This is the fault known as **toe pushing**!

Toe pushing and how to avoid it

Toe pushing is the error that occurs when you literally push with your toe picks rather than the whole of your blade. It is one of the most common faults in ice skating.

The result of using this pushing technique amounts to the skate making rather a lot of noise, poking little holes in the ice pad and giving highly inefficient forward stroking. So, in order to avoid this problem when forward stroking, make sure that your weight is centred along the pushing foot. This foot must be turned out at right angles to the direction of travel. If you follow these instructions, your picks will be unable to catch in the ice.

N.B. Toe pushing does not occur whilst skating backwards — which may be a relief to those who have this fault when skating forwards.

Now, if you feel ready to move on to the next stage of backward pushing, follow the instructions given in the next section.

Stage 3: backwards or backward skating on one foot

Stand with your feet together and turn the toes inwards

to form an inverted letter V. Bend both knees, press on the insides of your feet and push your heels outwards. When your feet are approximately eighteen inches apart, turn the heels inwards and, just before you draw them back together, lift the right foot off the ice. Place the heel of this foot in front of the toe of the skating foot and hold it in front for a couple of seconds, then place it back on the ice at the side of the skating foot. Repeat with the left foot.

At first, I can guarantee that this will seem quite difficult, but keep going and after a while you will see some real progress. The Stage 3: backwards is extremely important as it is the basis for much of your backwards skating and further progress is largely dependent upon it.

Being realistic, allow several skating sessions to learn this move and when you are able to hold the free leg in front for at least two seconds, you will be ready to try Stage 4: backwards as described in the next chapter. There is little point in trying the next stage until you have mastered this one — so good luck!

N.B. As with all backwards skating, make sure that you are aware of all potential hazards. This means anybody skating near to you. Turn around in both directions between pushes to make sure that the way is clear.

SUMMARY

This chapter assumes that many skaters will have bought their own equipment. It starts out dealing with any necessary adjustments to the fitting of the blades to the boots to suit the individual.

Your dealer will have fitted them as accurately as possible but every skater has a personal preference regarding the exact positioning of the blades. Bearing this in mind, most blades have two slot holes in both the sole and the heel plates of the skates.

The blades should have been attached to the boot at these four points, the slots enabling the blade to be moved slightly to either the inside or the outside.

A good test for accurate positioning is for the skater to push off, using the Stage 4: forward stroking technique. The skater must be travelling along in a straight line with both edges on the ice. Should the blade pull to either the left or the right, it may need to be moved slightly. If it pulls towards the inside edge, it should generally be moved slightly to the outside of the boot. If it pulls to the outside edge, it may need to be moved to the inside of the boot.

If the blade runs well, leave it and fit the remaining screws. Before making any radical changes yourself consult an expert. After every trip to the ice rink, check that your blades are still tightly fastened to the boots. Carry a screwdriver in your skate bag.

The next section deals with forward glides. Aim at the barrier and take three pushes, gliding on to the right foot, followed by the left and then the right. Keeping both edges in contact with the ice, hold the position with the arms out to the side and the free leg stretched out behind. Repeat with the other foot.

Toe pushing or pushing with the picks is a common error at this point. The effect of this amounts to a great deal of noise, unattractive free leg positioning and inefficient pushing.

To remedy this fault, make sure that the pushing foot is turned out at right angles to the skating foot and that the weight is on the ball of that pushing foot.

Stage 3: backwards involves standing as in the earlier stages with the feet forming an inverted V. The toes must be touching. Bend both knees and, pressing on the insides of the feet, push the heels outwards at the same time and with the same speed. Pull the heels back together and, just before they touch, lift one foot off the ice and place it so that the heel is lined in front of the toe of the other foot. Hold it there for several seconds.

Bring the feet back together and repeat with the other side. This is one of the most important methods of backward skating.

9 *Lesson Four*

By now you will have sorted out the correct positioning of your blades and will no doubt be breaking in your boots quite nicely.

As I said in the last chapter, they will seem rather stiff at first, so expect the whole adjustment process to take about a dozen visits to complete. Should you have any great difficulties dealing with this adjustment, refer back to the early part of the last chapter. Do make sure that your boots are loosely fastened. I often tell my students to leave the top hook unfastened at this stage, but this decision is up to you.

It should be said that as time goes by, your boots will soften and mould to your feet and, as this happens, you will need to tighten up the laces a little more.

In this chapter I am going to cover several new moves which are based upon your current knowledge of outside and inside edges. The first move that I am going to cover is called the **forward outside curve**. This is exactly what it appears to be, a curve on an outside edge, moving forward. Follow the instructions given below.

Forward outside curves

Find a hockey circle, or try to imagine a circle with a diameter of about 6 metres or 20 feet and stand on the edge facing in a clockwise direction (you can skate a much smaller circle too). Place your feet in such a way as to form a letter L. The heels should be together with your right foot and arm leading. You are going to be using the Stage 4: forward push.

Take three pushes, gliding on to the right foot, followed by the left and finally the right again.

Stretch the free leg back behind your skating foot and lean into the circle by stretching the whole of the free side of your body. Keep the free leg in position for five seconds (or as long as you can).

Forward outside curve. Sometimes it helps if you bring the free leg in front, as shown here

As with all new moves, you are unlikely to be able to do this immediately, so it would be realistic to allow several skating sessions to achieve the desired effect. N.B. At this point, if you can curve at all you are doing extremely well.

Now let's try the other foot.

Start as before but with the following changes. Firstly, face in an anticlockwise direction around the real or imagined hockey circle, with the left foot and arm leading. Glide on to the left foot, followed by the right and then the left again. Stretch the free side of the body (the right). Hold the position.

Do make sure that you are standing on a slightly bent knee during each curve. Practise these curves on each foot.

Now that you have tried a difficult curve, let's move on to one that for most people tends to be easier. This is the **forward inside curve** and you will find that the instructions given below are similar to those given for the outside curves, although there are a few specific changes.

Forward inside curves

Forward inside curve. You can also finish with the free foot in front, as shown in the diagram

Stand on your real or imagined hockey circle, facing in a clockwise direction. The left foot should be leading along with the right arm. Glide on to the left, then the right, then finally the left. Turn out and stretch the free leg behind. Lean into the circle by way of stretching up the skating side of the body (the left). Bend the skating knee and hold the edge for as long as possible. Let's try the other side.

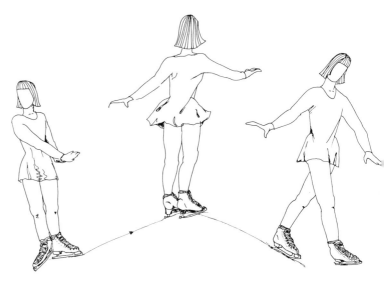

Face in an anticlockwise direction with the right foot and the left arm leading. Take three pushes, on to the right foot, followed by the left and then the right again. Lean towards the centre of your circle, by stretching up the right side (skating side) of your body, and follow the instructions as for the left foot.

Practise these edges until you feel reasonably confident. Be aware of your posture at all times as your body must be held up straight along with your head; and remember to keep your skating knee bent!

The next section deals with **forward crossovers**. Forward crossovers amount to a combination of edges and pushes which enable you to turn corners and change direction pushing at the same time.

Forward crossovers

Crossovers amount to a combination of an outside edge on one foot followed by an inside on the other, with the change of foot being made by way of a crossover movement.

As with all skating moves, crossovers can be skated in either direction, but for the sake of this section, we are going to start with those moving in an anticlockwise direction.

Stand with your feet together and the knees bent. Bring your right arm forwards and glide on to an outside edge on the left foot, keeping that knee slightly bent. Lift and cross the right foot over the left and place it down next to the left on an inside edge. To complete the move, stretch the left foot back and then place it down next to the right. Repeat.

Forward crossover

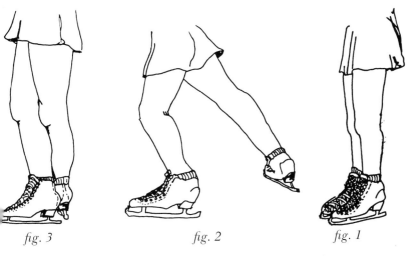

fig. 3   fig. 2   fig. 1

You may well notice that should you push and place your feet on the relevant edges, you will be turning in an anticlockwise direction, and if you complete a series of these crossovers, you will come back to where you started. You will have skated a circle of crossovers.

When you have acquired the feel of this direction, you should try the other side. For most people the other side presents more difficulties. This is due to the fact that most people are right handed and naturally turn in an anticlockwise direction.

Stand with the feet together, the left arm leading and the knees slightly bent.

Glide on to an outside edge on the right foot . . . *curve* . . . and stretch the free leg back. Lift the free foot across the skating foot and place it down on an inside edge, then, to complete the move stretch the right foot back and place it down next to the left. Repeat.

Practise these crossovers until you feel that you have control; in fact it's a good idea, if the rink is reasonably empty, to move into the centre and complete a circle in one direction, followed immediately by one in the other direction, by way of clockwise and anticlockwise crossovers. The result should be a figure-of-eight pattern, and apart from being good fun, is a good practical exercise for changing from one direction to the other.

When you feel comfortable skating the Stage 3: backwards pushes as described in the last chapter, you will be ready to try **Stage 4: backwards or backward glides**.

If, on the other hand, they are still causing you some problems, continue to practise the Stage 3: backwards until you are able to glide for a couple of seconds on each foot.

For those of you who feel ready, let's try the Stage 4: backwards.

Stage 4: backwards or backward glides
As with all the previous sections that have dealt with

backward skating, start off by placing your feet together, then bend your knees and turn your toes inwards to form an inverted letter V position. (As with the forward glides you will be giving three pushes, holding the position after the final push.)

The heel of your free foot must be positioned in line with the toe of the skating foot on the end of each push.

Press on your inside edges and push the feet apart at the same time as making sure they are moving away at the same time and with the same speed.

Glide on to the right foot and lift the left in front, followed by the left and finally the right again. You will end up standing on the right foot with the left in front. If you don't, you have started on the wrong foot!

The free foot, the left, should be held in line with the skating foot. See photo.

Hold this position for as long as possible, making sure that both edges of the skate are on the ice. The result of this should be a backward glide in a straight line standing on the right foot.

Backward glide

In order to maintain your balance and control, you must keep the skating knee slightly bent and on the end of each glide, remember to bring your feet back together.

Try the other foot, bearing in mind the following information. Repeat the instructions as described for the right foot, but glide on to the left first, followed by the right and then finally the left.

Don't be surprised if you have some initial problems when it comes to making the skate glide backwards in a straight line. This is perfectly normal and you will soon overcome any of these difficulties with a little practice. (Should you find that you are not moving in a straight line, you will have caught an edge.)

N.B. As I have said in each section dealing with backward skating, do check that your skating direction is clear of other skaters before starting these or any other backward moves. Continue to check whilst practising.

If some other skater appears to be a likely hazard, put both feet down and bend your knees slightly to make sure that you keep in control and avoid any potential collision. Bearing in mind these occasional situations when drastic action is required, the next section deals with how you can **stop when skating backwards**.

How to stop when skating backwards

Stopping while skating backwards involves using the snow plough method mentioned in the Lesson One, only from backwards.

Keeping your feet slightly apart, bend your knees, pressing on your inside edges at the same time pushing the feet apart as you do so.

SUMMARY

This chapter deals with several topics. If you are

having any problems with your new skating boots, this is normal. Loosen them and leave the top hook unfastened. If there are still problems, refer back to the beginning of the previous chapter.

The next section deals with outside edges. Using a hockey circle as a guide, stand on the edge. If you are going to practise the right foot face in a clockwise direction and if it's going to be the left, face anticlockwise. When on the right foot, lead with the right arm; when on the left, lead with the left. Take three pushes starting and finishing with the relevant foot. Lean into the circle so that your skate tilts over to the outside. The simplest method of attaining your body lean is by way of stretching up the whole of the free side of your body, whilst skating outside edges, and lowering the free side whilst skating inside edges. Your free leg must be stretched out behind with the foot turned away from you.

The next area deals with inside edges. Stand on your hockey circle. If you are going to practise the left foot, face clockwise and for the right anticlockwise. When you stand on the left foot, the right must lead and when on the right, the left. Take three pushes and lean into the circle. The free leg must be stretched back with the free foot turned away from you.

The next section covers forward crossovers. This is the movement which enables skaters to turn corners while pushing. Crossovers amount to a combination of an outside followed by an inside edge, caused by crossing one foot over the other. For most people, the most natural direction is anticlockwise.

Stand with the feet together, the right arm leading and push on to an outside edge on the left. Keep the skating knee bent and then lift the right foot across and place it down on an inside edge next to the left. Stretch the left foot back and place it at the side of the right and repeat. For the other direction, glide on to the right foot with the left arm leading. Cross the left foot over. Lift the right foot off and place it at the side of the right. Repeat.

To be able to attempt Stage 4: backward glides, you must be completely confident of Stage 3. Backward glides involve taking three pushes, all in a line, lifting the relevant free foot in front and holding it there for as long as possible. Both edges should be in contact with the ice. At the end of each glide, the feet must be brought back together.

Stopping whilst skating backwards is achieved by standing with the feet apart, bending the knees and pushing the skates out sideways, both at the same time.

10 *Lesson Five*

On your fifth visit to the ice rink, you will have become extremely familiar with all the systems operating in your rink.

All being well your new boots and skates will be breaking in and you may have to tighten them up a little more than on previous visits, as they mould to fit your feet. It may even be possible to reduce the amount of protection needed, although you would be well advised to continue to take along some padding and plasters in your skate bag, just in case your enthusiasm gets the better of you.

As with all other sessions, your first priority must be to warm up your body. Start by practising some forward and backward skating, then move on to the simpler moves as your body warms up and you start to get the feel of the ice. Then move on to the more difficult elements.

Concentrate on your posture. Make sure that your body is held straight and definitely not leaning forwards. Your head must be held up in line with your shoulders, hips and skating foot. The arms should be held out to the side at about waist level.

Always bend your knees before pushing and keep the skating knee slightly relaxed with the free leg straight and stretched out behind you.

N.B. On all backwards steps, the free leg should lift up with the toe turned slightly outwards. The free leg must be kept straight.

This chapter deals with some rather advanced moves, which as you can imagine, are dependent upon your ability to perform those already covered in the previous four chapters.

The first move that we are going to cover is **Stage 5: backwards or backward outside curves**.

Before going any further, if you are still having difficulty with your backward glides or indeed any of the earlier stages, it would be wise to leave this next section until you feel completely happy with the more basic backward moves. If you can skate the backward glides with a degree of comfort, you should move on to this section.

The last chapter dealt with the forward outside curves and they have much in common with the backward curves, with a couple of major differences. These are firstly, the fact that you are going backwards instead of forwards and secondly, the position of the free foot. This foot is held in front when skating backwards.

Stage 5: backwards or backward outside curves

The right foot

Stand on your real or imagined circle facing in a clockwise direction with your right foot leading along with the right arm pulled back behind you and your left arm in front. See diagram.

Look back towards the direction in which you are going to travel. Bend both knees and glide on to your right foot, bring the feet together and glide on to the left, followed by a final glide on to the right again. Lift the free foot and place it in line with the toe of the skating foot. You should now be standing with the free leg in front (not too high, please). Stretch the free side (the left) of your body slightly and lean inwards. Make sure your skating knee is bent!

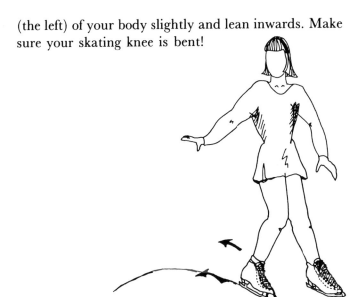

Hold this position for as long as you can, then, when you feel that you cannot hold on any longer or you run out of speed, bring your feet back together and repeat the move.

N.B. At first, in order to gain sufficient speed, you may need to take five pushes instead of three.

Backward outside curve showing the starting position

The left foot

The instructions that apply to the left foot are similar to those already given for the right with a few specific changes, which relate to the direction in which you will be travelling, along with the arm positions and the skating foot.

Start by facing in an anticlockwise direction on your circle.

Your right arm should be in front and the left arm pulled back. Turn your head so that you are looking towards the direction in which you will be travelling.

Bend both knees. Push on to the left foot followed by the right and then the left again. Hold the final position on the left foot (with the free side of your body stretched) for as long as possible.

If you can manage to curve even a little it will be worth your while trying the moves contained within the next sections. These deal with **backward crossovers**.

Backward crossovers

Backward crossovers are one of the main methods of moving backwards across the ice. As with most ice-skating steps, they can be skated in either clockwise or anticlockwise directions.

When you watch the top ice skaters going through their moves, you will see how often backward crossovers are used. For example it is usual to approach spins by way of backward crossovers and when a skater wishes to get up speed before jumping there is a good chance that backward crossovers will be used. The ice dancers too use them when warming up and frequently within their routines.

The first step involves a backward push on to an outside edge followed by a crossing over of the free foot which is then placed in contact with the ice on an inside edge. The last stage amounts to drawing back the original skating foot and placing it down beside the other one. If all this sounds complicated follow the instructions given below.

Stand again on your real or imagined circle with your feet together and your body facing clockwise around the circle. Look towards the direction in which you plan to travel. The left arm should be in front with the right arm held back in line with your skating foot (fig.1).

Bend both knees, then push and stand on the right foot (fig.2).

Keeping the skating knee bent, lift the free foot (the left), over the skating foot and place it down on the other side drawing your right foot back as you do so (fig. 3). Try the other side!

Stand as before but this time facing in an anticlockwise direction, with the left arm back and the right in front. Bend the knees, then push and glide backwards on to the left foot. Keep the skating knee bent, and cross the right foot over and place it down next to the left followed by a stretch back of the left foot, pushing with your outside edge as you do so. Repeat!

Make sure that you are looking towards the direction of travel with your knees slightly bent. Your pushing knee should straighten on the end of each step. As with the forward crossovers, should you continue to crossover in the same direction, you will complete a circle.

Backward crossover. Keep your skating knee bent

fig. 1

fig. 2

fig. 3

The three turn

The majority of skaters have a favourite direction to which they like to turn. Most people turn naturally to the left (anticlockwise) although a few prefer turning to the right.

This point can be easily observed during televised competitions as most of the participants will jump and spin turning anticlockwise as they do so. That is why most rinks organize their sessions so that the traffic direction in general skating follows this norm.

The **three turn** is one of the most basic turns used in ice skating. The name comes from the fact that this turn leaves a number 3-shaped tracing on the ice.

There are various types of three turn, some of which start from forwards and others from backwards. They can also originate from both outside and inside edges.

A three turn involves a 180-degree turn, which for the sake of this book will start from a forward outside edge. The turn is completed on one foot, but the direction and edge change after the turn. Therefore, if you start the turn on an outside edge forwards, you will end up on an inside edge backwards.

The three turn, starting on the right foot

The first three turn is to be that which starts on the right foot, so have a look at the instructions and diagram and try it.

Stand on your (hockey) circle facing forwards in a clockwise direction. Bend both knees and place your right arm in front, then push on to the right foot on an outside edge. Make sure you are standing on a reasonably bent knee, then change your arms so that the left arm and shoulder comes in front of you.

Bring your free foot against the skating foot, keeping it off the ice and straighten up the skating knee a little as you do so. As you turn press the left shoulder back to check your rotation. All being well, you should end up backwards on an inside edge, having completed a half turn.

The instructions applicable to the other side are much the same. Stand on the circle facing in an anticlockwise direction, with the left arm leading, then bend both knees and glide on to the left foot.

Follow the circle and bring the right arm and shoulder forward. Place the free foot against the skating foot, straighten up the skating knee slightly, then take the right arm and shoulder back to check your rotation. As with the right foot you should now be travelling backwards on the same foot.

SUMMARY

This chapter covers the fifth stage in your skating development. At this point you would be well advised to perfect the moves learned in the earlier sections before attempting those covered in this chapter.

If you are unable to skate backwards without great difficulty, you should spend this session revising the Stage 4: backwards.

Be aware of your posture. Ensure that you bend your knees when pushing. The skating knee must be bent and the free leg turned out and stretched behind, as well as being straight.

Stage 5: backwards (or backward outside curves) involve a similar technique to that used for the forward outside.

Stand on a hockey circle. If you are going to practise

the left foot, face in an anticlockwise direction around the circle. When practising the right, face clockwise. You should have your opposite arm in front.

Take three pushes starting on the relevant foot. After the third, hold the free leg in front and lean into the circle.

The next section deals with backward crossovers. They are similar to forward crossovers, inasmuch as the movement involves lifting one foot and crossing it over the other. The first push is from an outside edge and the second from an inside.

The forward outside three turn amounts to a turn starting from a forward outside edge and, after completing a 180-degree turn on the same foot, travelling backwards on an inside edge. The turn is achieved by a combination of turning the body and lifting the weight slightly by way of raising the skating knee.

11 *Lesson Six*

This chapter assumes that you are confident performing all the moves covered in the previous five lessons. Your forwards and backwards skating should be coming along quite well and as for your edges, they must be coming along quite well too!

The first area that I am going to cover relates to **changing direction**. This can be achieved either by stepping from backwards to forwards or from forwards to backwards. The best place to start this exercise is via stepping from backwards to forwards and the next section deals with this in some detail.

Stepping from backwards to forwards

Start this move by using the technique referred to in the section on backward glides in chapter 9. This is because you are going to start out by skating a backward glide and then, whilst gliding along, you are going to turn your body through 180 degrees and step to forwards on the other foot.

First of all, start with the right foot. You should be standing with your feet together and your arms held out to the side, in line with your shoulders with your knees slightly bent.

Glide on to the right foot, at the same time as lifting the free foot in front. Bring your feet back together and glide on to the left and finally the right (fig.1). Standing with the left foot in front, take your left shoulder back and turn your head in the same direction. Place your heels together (fig.2) and step forwards on to an outside edge on the left foot, drawing back the right shoulder as you do so (fig.3). Hold the forward outside edge!

For the left foot, follow the aforementioned instructions, the glide backwards on to the left foot, followed by the right and then the left again. Hold the right foot in front and take your right shoulder back. Turn your head over your right shoulder to face forwards, bringing your heels together at the same time. Push forwards on to an outside edge on the right foot, drawing the left shoulder back at the same time. Hold the position as long as you can.

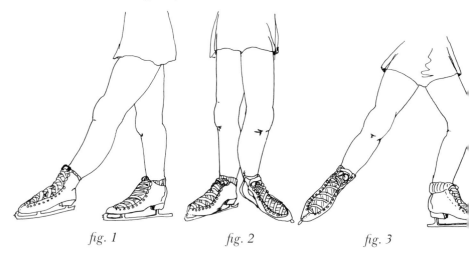

fig. 1   *fig. 2*   *fig. 3*

When you feel more confident with these turns, you should move on to the **Mohawk turn**. A Mohawk is a turn which usually involves turning from forwards to backwards, changing feet at the same time. Both the entry and exit edges are the same, either outside or inside. So should you start off on an inside edge forwards, you will end up on an inside edge skating backwards.

The Mohawk we are going to cover (and probably the easiest) is that starting from a forward inside edge.

Forward inside Mohawk

Starting on the right foot

Stand on your real or imagined hockey circle, facing in an anticlockwise direction. The left arm and right foot should be leading.

Bend both knees, and glide on to the right foot, bending the skating knee as you do so (fig.1). Bring your feet together so that the heel of the free foot is placed to the middle of your instep. The effect of this will cause your feet to form a letter T shape (fig.2). Bring your right shoulder in front, so that it is in line with your skating foot, and change feet, by way of lifting up your right foot and stepping on to your left foot. Press the right shoulder back to check your rotation, then hold the back edge for as long as possible, or a couple of seconds (fig.3).

Right foot forward inside Mohawk

fig. 3 *fig. 2*

fig. 1

Starting on the left foot:

For the left foot, stand on your hockey circle facing in a clockwise direction. Your right arm must be leading. Glide on to the left foot, bringing the heel of the right foot to the middle of the left, to form your letter T shape. Bring your left shoulder forward so that it is in line with the skating foot then lift off the left foot, so that you are travelling backwards on the right. Press the left shoulder back to check the rotation.

Forward outside to inside change of edge or serpentine

The last area that I am going to cover relates to changing from an outside to an inside edge on the same foot.

A change of edge involves rolling the skate over from one edge to the other and this is accomplished by altering the body lean.

When you are skating using the Stage 4: forward-stroking movement, you may notice that each time you bring your feet together, your skating foot will roll over towards the inside. This roll (a change of edge), is essential if the next push is to be made from that foot (from the inside edge). When we are skating, we are constantly pushing on to one foot and then changing edge, as that foot becomes the pushing force.

The right foot

Change from forward outside edge to inside

At its simplest the tracing formed by a change of edge resembles a letter S. Let's try it.

Stand on your hockey circle and face in a clockwise direction, with the right foot and arm leading.

Bend both knees and push on to a forward outside curve on the right foot. As you approach the halfway point place your free leg, the left, in front, so that it is forward in line with your skating foot. Take the free leg back and change your arms, so that the left comes forwards. The free leg should be stretched back with the free foot turned outwards, and you will be gliding along on an inside edge. Remember to keep the relevant skating side stretched at all times, then when you feel reasonably comfortable with this move, you should try the left foot.

N.B. As you bring the free foot in front, make sure that it touches the skating foot as it passes.

The left foot

Facing in an anticlockwise direction, stand on your hockey circle with your left foot and arm leading. Bend and glide on to a forward outside edge on this foot. When you have travelled nearly halfway around the circle, place the free leg in front then draw it back, turning out the free foot as you do so. Lean into your circle and repeat.

SUMMARY

This chapter covers several topics. The first section covers stepping from backwards to forwards. Start as for backward glides. If gliding on to the right foot, take three pushes, and hold the left leg in front, standing on a bent knee. Take the left shoulder back and bring the feet close together. Turn to face forwards and push on to the left foot. Take the right shoulder back slightly and hold on a forward outside edge. If you are gliding on to the left foot, take three pushes, and hold the right foot in front. Take the right shoulder back and bring the heels together. Turn your head in the same direction and push forwards on to an outside edge on the right foot. Draw the left shoulder back at the same time.

The next section deals with forward Mohawks.

Mohawks are turns which involve 180-degree turns, by way of changing feet, but not edge. This chapter refers to the forward inside Mohawk. For the right foot, stand with that foot leading along with the left arm facing in an anticlockwise direction. Push on to an inside edge on the right, turning out the back foot. Bring the heel of that foot to the inside of the skating foot and the right shoulder forward. Change feet, stepping down on a backward inside edge on the left foot.

For the left foot, face in a clockwise direction, the right arm leading and push. Turn out the free foot and place the heel to the middle of the skating foot and change feet. The last area deals with the change of edge. Start with the same arm as skating foot, changing the arm as the free leg draws back after the change.

This amounts to pushing on to an outside edge, drawing the free foot forward and taking it back leaning towards an inside edge as you do so.

12 *Free Skating and Compulsory Figures*

Many of you will know from watching television that free skating amounts to jumps, spins and positions interconnected by way of intricate joining steps performed to music.

Some people see free skating as a sport, others as an art form. Personally, I believe this discipline to be a superb combination of the two.

This is one area which has progressed at a staggering rate; in fact you don't have to go back a long way to find the technical content of some of the free-skating programmes very different from that expected from the skater of the 1990s.

Back in the mid-seventies, a double axel jump was often the most technically demanding jump required of the top female competitors, whereas today there are quite a few skaters performing triple axels and more! (A double axel is a jump which involves the skater making two and a half revolutions in the air, taking off on a forward outside edge and landing on a backward outside, whereas the triple contains three and a half turns with the same take off and landing.)

There have been some really great free skaters in the last twenty years, such as John Curry and Robin Cousins of the U.K. and Toller Cranston, Brian Orser and Kurt Browning of Canada. All of these skaters have contributed greatly to the technical and artistic developments of the sport.

The girls have included such superb skaters as

Debbie Dorothy Hamill and Debbie Thomas of the U.S. and
Thomas, the great Katterina Witt of Germany.
USA, 1986   The girls are now obliged to complete the most
World difficult of triple jumps and this fact alone demonstrates
Champion remarkable technical progress.

Now that the compulsory figures have been taken out of the championships, the standard of free skating looks set to soar even higher, with the additional practice time that this change allows the competitors.

However, that's for the future. We should concern ourselves with a few introductory moves that you can try, so if you feel like being a little adventurous, read on!

The next few sections deal with a couple of simple free-skating moves. Before trying to jump, please read through the section dealing with the 'Stand spin and test for natural spinning direction', as you must find out in which direction you turn naturally and, as a result, from which foot you should be jumping.

Before going any further, it is important to note that in order to attempt any of the basic jumps and spins, you must have good balance along with reasonable forward and backward skating. In addition you should be able to skate three turns and Mohawks in both directions (along with feeling confident as you do so).

N.B. Confidence is one of the most important requirements in skating!

The first area that we are going to cover is **how to spin**. The technique of spinning will also enable you to work out two things. Firstly, in which direction you should spin, and as a result, in which direction you should turn naturally. This is because it is usual to spin and jump turning towards the same direction. The skater who can jump and spin to a high level in both directions is a rarity.

Although most people turn to the left, or anticlockwise, you may be one of the small number who prefer the other direction. If you wish to find out which is the best for you follow the instructions in the next section. N.B. Many left-handed people prefer to spin in a clockwise direction.

Stand spin and test for natural spinning direction

The first spin that you are going to try involves the use of the right foot.

Stand with your feet about eighteen inches apart and the right toe in the ice. Take your right shoulder back as far as you can, then using your right toe, push yourself round to the left, bringing your right shoulder slightly forward at the same time as lifting your right foot up against your left knee.

Draw your arms together to keep up the momentum of your spin. If you find that you can turn reasonably easily, good. Now try the other direction, by placing your left toe in the ice and taking your left shoulder back as far as possible. Push from your left toe, lifting the left foot up against your right knee and bringing the left shoulder slightly forward.

Try each direction a couple of times, and you will soon find out which is the natural direction for you. If you have problems deciding which is the best direction for you, practise both ways until you can make a decision then stick to it.

Jumps

Virtually all jumps performed on ice involve turning in the air and the use of only one leg to obtain sufficient height and time to make the necessary rotations for the particular move. The majority of jumps take off from backwards either from edges or directly off the toe picks. Some jumps require a change of foot on the landing and others are rather like hops, taking off and landing on the same foot.

Nearly all jumps land backwards and on an outside edge. (When performing all jumps, whether on or off the ice, the last part of the foot to leave the ice is the toe.)

To find out which foot you should be using for take

off and in which direction you should be turning, please follow the instructions given in the section above relating to spinning.

When you have discovered which is your ideal spinning direction, you will be able to pick the appropriate take-off foot in accordance with the requirements of the particular jump.

Let's assume that you spin to the left, in which case you will also jump in that direction, and try the **Three** or **Waltz jump**, as it is called by some people.

Three or waltz jump

The three jump is one of the few forward take-off jumps as well as being one of the most basic. This jump starts from a forward outside edge on one foot, makes a half turn in the air, and then lands on a backward outside edge on the other foot.

With the left arm leading, strike on to a strong forward outside edge on your left foot, bending the skating knee and stretching the free leg back at the same time.

As you take off, bring the free leg through in front of the skating leg, along with the right shoulder. Land backwards on the right foot with the arms held out around waist level, taking the free leg behind as you do so. You should be travelling on a backward outside edge. If you are not you should repeat the move.

If you feel that you should be jumping from the right foot, on the basis that you are a clockwise spinner, strike on to that foot with the right arm slightly forward, then bring the free leg through, along with the left shoulder and land on that foot (the left).

When you have tried both the stand spin and the three jump, you should move on to try a **spiral**.

This is an extremely effective move, sometimes called an **arabesque** and what's more it's great fun and frequently used in free-skating programmes. Spirals can be skated either backwards or forwards on either edge. Let's take the most basic and as such the next section deals with a forward outside spiral.

Specific instructions will be given for those who prefer to turn in an anticlockwise direction (the majority of skaters). This means the left foot!

Spiral

Approach this move by way of forward crossovers moving in an anticlockwise direction. Your arms should be held out at about waist level. When you have completed three or four crossovers push on to the left foot and lean forward at the same time as lifting up your free leg. You should arrive at a position where your head and free leg are in line, with the arms held out and head up, standing on a straight skating knee.

The free leg must be straight with the free foot turned outwards.

Should you prefer to turn to the right, enter the move by way of clockwise forward crossovers, and spiral on the right foot.

Joanne Conway, 1990 British Champion

The drag

A drag is an effective yet simple move, one of the few

that most people can learn to perform pretty well instantaneously.

Hold the arms out level with your shoulders and skate forwards, taking three steps as follows, left, right, left. Bend the skating knee (the left) and stretch the free leg back (the right) behind you, keeping the foot in contact with the ice. You should continue to bend your skating knee until it is down as low as possible. The inside of your right boot should be dragging along the ice.

For the right foot follow the same instructions starting with that foot.

More advanced free-skating moves

More advanced free-skating moves are certainly beyond the scope of this book.

Should you wish to learn more about free skating, you should consider employing the services of a suitably qualified professional skating coach.

Some people may like to wear crash pads (to protect your bum) and possibly shin, knee and elbow protectors. All of these things are available from larger sports equipment stores. Generally, jogging trousers and long-sleeved shirts will provide adequate protection.

Your first competition

When you have been skating for a while and can perform a few jumps and spins along with a few dance steps, your coach may well suggest that you enter your first competition.

To be able to take part you will need a routine of several minutes in length in accordance with the relevant competition rules, incorporating all of your current skills.

When the competition comes around, it will be necessary for you to travel to the competition rink. (The rink will have organized practice times for all the competitors.)

When the time comes around for your particular event, the first six or so will be asked to go on to the ice for a warm-up. If you are amongst this group, you will be expected to skate around in order to get the feel of the ice before you skate your programme for the judges.

After a couple of minutes the referee will blow a whistle and call everybody off the ice. The competition is about to start.

The judges will be sitting close to the ice with boxes containing their marks hung around their necks. (If the rink is really hi-tec, there may be an electronic scoreboard ready to display the marks as soon as they are awarded.)

You will then step on to the ice and skate over to your starting place, probably hearing your friends and supporters clapping and yelling to encourage you.

Your music will start and off you go, spinning and jumping around the ice until you finish your programme.

You hear more clapping and yelling from your friends and skate to the side, where your coach will be waiting to greet you.

A moment later you will hear a whistle blow and then turn to see the judges standing up holding scores for your programme. There are black and red numbers. You know that the black numbers mean whole marks and the red, tenths of marks. The judges will then put their score cards back into the boxes and then the referee will blow the whistle again.

Again the judges will draw out their score cards, only this time the marks represent their opinions of your artistic impression rather than technical merit, which was the first score.

I wonder if you won!

Compulsory figures

Compulsory figures are the geometrical patterns

formed on the ice by the skater using various edges and turns. The intention is to produce accurate representations consisting of either two or three circles.

The skater is required to skate over or 'trace' these circles either two or three more times according to the figure to be skated.

Many experts believe the compulsory figures to be the basis of all skating, as they do give great insight into and control of the edges.

For many years the figures formed a major part of all international free-skating competitions, although they were excluded from the 1990−1 season onwards.

The next section deals with the basic **forward outside eight**. (The name comes from the fact that two circles joined together do rather resemble a basic conception of the number 8.)

Forward outside eight

*Forward
outside eight*

Stand on a fixed point on the ice. This could be any small area of the ice that is different in shading from the rest, or a hockey mark. It is known as the 'centre'.

Facing down the rink, put both feet together. If you are going to skate on to the left foot, your left arm must be in front. If you are pushing on to the right foot, make sure that the right arm is leading. Turn out both feet and slide them into a letter T position with either foot leading. Bend both knees and push on to the leading foot, stretching the free leg back and bending the skating knee at the same time.

The moment your skate touches the ice you should stretch your skating side, the same side as the foot you are standing on, and lean into the circle. Try to be aware of your starting point, or 'centre', so you judge where you are and how far you have to travel.

When you are beyond the halfway point bring the free leg in front. You should now be standing with the heel of the free foot in front of the toe of the skating foot. Hold this position until you are back at your starting point (centre). On returning to your centre, bring the feet together and repeat with the other foot.

N.B. The suggested positions can vary slightly according to individual preference.

SUMMARY

This chapter covers some of the basic free-skating moves. The first section deals with two areas: how to spin, and how to find out which is your natural spinning and jumping direction. You should spin and jump in the same direction.

Stand with your feet 18 inches apart, with the right toe in the ice, the right shoulder pulled back, and the arms held out. Push from your toe at the same time as bringing the right shoulder in front, lift the right foot up against your skating knee and hold your arms together. This sequence of moves will make you spin to the left, which is the direction in which most people naturally turn. You should also try the other direction, and compare the two, that which feels easier is the one for you.

Once you have decided in which direction you are going to spin, you will also be able to work out which is the best direction for jumping. This is because most skaters spin and jump in the same direction.

Nearly all jumps performed by ice skaters involve turning during the move, if there is more than one turn, the jump will be described as being a double, triple or quadruple, according to the number.

The next section deals with the Three Jump or Waltz Jump.

This is a jump from a forward outside edge on one foot to a backward outside edge on the other. A half turn is made in the air. If you spin towards the left, anticlockwise, you should push off on to the left foot, and jump to the right foot, ensuring that you land backwards on an outside edge. The free leg lifts up in front of the skating leg on the take-off and stretches back behind the skating leg on the landing.

The last section deals with a forward spiral. This is a move where the skater is gliding along with the free leg in line with the body and as high as the head.

Skate three or four anticlockwise crossovers forwards. Holding the arms out and standing on a straight left leg, lean forwards, lifting your free leg as you do so. Your head must be held up and the free leg straight and turned out.

If you prefer to turn to the right, skate your forward crossovers in a clockwise direction and spiral on your right foot.

The drag involves holding the arms out level with the shoulders, then skating forward on one foot, bending the skating knee and stretching the free leg back, keeping it in contact with the ice and dragging the inside of that foot along.

Although the compulsory figures are no longer included in the championships, largely due to pressure from TV audiences who feel they are boring to watch, for many people they remain the basis of the sport. Control of both edges backwards and forwards is essential to your progress.

Compulsory figures are geometrical patterns consisting of either two or three circles, along with various turns and loop patterns forming part of the tracing.

It should be said that a great deal of practice and control is needed in order to feel comfortable on these moves.

13 *Ice Dancing*

How often have you been riveted to your TV set by the speed and style of the great ice dancers? Let's face it, who can listen to Ravel's 'Bolero' and not think of Torvill and Dean?

Ice dancing is always one of the most popular audience events in the international skating year and perhaps this is due to the speed and grace of the skaters moving in perfect unison across the ice.

In its most basic form, this discipline amounts to the performance (usually with a partner) of steps and positions to music of a regular tempo interpreting dances of particular characters.

The ice-dancing events in international competitions are divided into three sections, the **Compulsory Dances**, the **Original Rhythm Dance** and the **Free Dance**. The first section involves the compulsories.

Compulsory dances

These dances amount to sequences of skating steps which were devised by various ice dance experts over several generations and approved by the governing bodies of the sport.

The compulsory dances form the basis of the test systems.

The majority of the dances have their origins in ballroom-type dancing — waltzes, foxtrots, tangos and so on. Each has its own specific character, which the skaters are required to convey to the judges. Some of these dances will require a complete circuit of the rink on each sequence, whereas others will only use half a circuit before repeating. Many of the dances were invented by the British experts of the 1930s. There are particular patterns that must be skated.

In any given competition or test, all skaters will be required to skate the dance exactly as laid down by the rules of the International Skating Union and repeat the sequence twice more.

The original-rhythm dance

The second section is called the Original-Rhythm Dance. This is an original routine devised by each competing couple which interprets whatever tempo and character (quickstep, tango, waltz, etc.) has been set down in the rules for that competition.

Although the routine has a duration of two minutes (give or take ten seconds), the couple are free to move around the ice in either direction with only a few restrictions. These amount to a maximum of two pieces of music and the fact that the skaters are not allowed to include lifts of any kind.

The free dance

The third section is called the Free Dance. This is a routine lasting up to four minutes (three minutes for junior and four minutes for senior events) which enables the skaters to show off their technical and artistic skills relating to footwork, small low lifts (unlike the pair skaters with their overhead lifts), general originality and ability to interpret their music.

Unlike the Original Rhythm Dance, the skaters are allowed to use additional pieces of music of varying character with no restrictions being placed on the theme that they choose to interpret. This naturally enough gives the skaters considerable scope to express themselves.

Can anybody ice dance?

If this area of the sport appeals to you and you would like to try it out for yourself you must have achieved a minimum level of competence in your general skating. By this I mean you must be able to skate forwards and backwards along with other skills such as forward and backward crossovers (crosscuts), forward three turns, Mohawks on each foot, etc.

I have included a couple of dances in this chapter for those of you who would like to practise some simple forward skating but still feel unsure of the turns.

N.B. Anything more advanced will require professional instruction.

How do I start?

Find out when there are ice-dancing sessions at your local rink. There may be classes on particular days and it would be a good idea to join in to learn even the basic moves.

After a while you should employ a good ice-dancing teacher, preferably of the opposite sex (the rink will be able to advise you in this department).

Start out by booking a couple of fifteen-minute lessons and see how you get on. You will soon learn the basic dances and then you can have a go to music.

Every couple will have slightly different skating problems and although there are many standard faults, such as not standing up straight, toe pushing, and being out of time with the beat of the music, it is much better for the coach to zoom in on a specific couple.

Ice dance steps that you need to know

Three dances are covered in this chapter and they are the **Dutch waltz, canasta tango** and the **preliminary foxtrot**. Before we can move on to any of the dances, you must be able to perform a couple of elementary steps. The first of these is called a **forward chasse**.

Forward chasse

Glide on to an outside edge on your left foot (fig.1). Bring your feet together and raise the left foot a couple of inches above the ice (figs. 2 & 3), so that you are standing on an inside edge on the right foot. Bring the feet back together and glide on to another outside edge on the left foot (figs. 4 & 5). The arms should be held out to the side with the hands at about waist height (unless you are doing this with a partner).

Forward chasse, starting on the left foot. Don't forget to lift your free foot

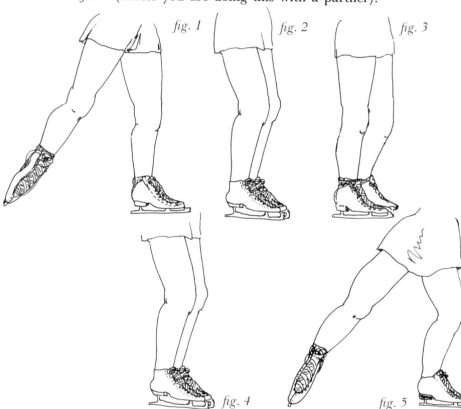

fig. 1   fig. 2   fig. 3
fig. 4   fig. 5

The **right-foot chasse** is completed in the same manner but starting on the right foot.

N.B. Please note that the length of time allowed for each step on any of the chasses covered in this chapter is dependent upon the dance being skated.

There is also a move called a **slide chasse**.

Slide chasse

Glide on to an outside edge on the left foot, stretching your free leg back. Bring your feet together and slide the left foot in front. You will now be standing on an inside edge. Bring the feet back together (see diagram). For the right foot, follow the instructions given above, starting on the right.

Slide chasse, starting on the left foot

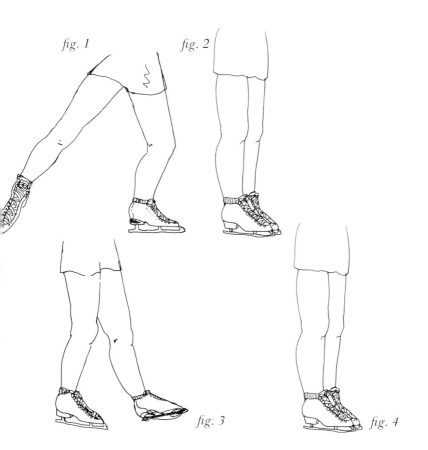

fig. 1   fig. 2

fig. 3   fig. 4

Forward run or progressive

The forward run involves a series of steps running either clockwise or anticlockwise. The first step is usually on to an outside edge, the second an inside.

On the second step the free foot is placed down on an inside edge, slightly in front and to the side of the skating foot. At the same time as this foot touches the ice the other foot is stretched back. Every step provides a push.

It is a good idea to practise these forward runs in a *Forward run* circle, continually repeating the steps.

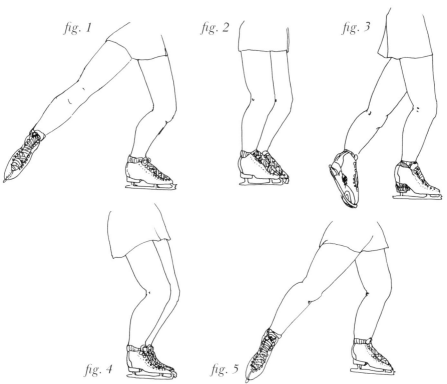

fig. 1   fig. 2   fig. 3

fig. 4   fig. 5

Swing roll

This move frequently appears in ice dancing, as it is an effective but easy step to perform.

Stand with your feet together, and bend both knees. Strike on to an outside edge on either foot, stretching the free leg back as you do so. Slowly straighten your skating knee at the same time as bringing the free leg in front. Bring the feet back together and push on to the other foot.

Cross roll and swing

This involves standing on an outside edge and then crossing the free foot over and placing it down on an outside edge, followed by a swing roll of the free foot.

The last step that we are going to look at is the **backward chasse**.

Backward chasse

Push backward on to an outside edge. Bring the feet together, then change feet, raising the free foot slightly as you do so. Bring the feet back together and repeat the first push.

For the left foot, follow these instructions, pushing on to the left foot first.

N.B. The first edge is an outside, the second is an inside.

As with the progressive runs, it is a good idea to practise several backward chasses in one direction around a circle.

Ice dance holds

The first is the **Kilian hold**, as this is used for both the Dutch waltz and the preliminary foxtrot and in reverse for the canasta tango.

Kilian hold

Both parties are facing in the same direction with the girl on the right hand side of the boy. The boy's right hand rests on the girl's right hip bone, held in place by her right hand.

The girl's left arm is straight and held out across the boy's upper body. The boy holds the girl's left hand with his left. The couple should be standing as close together as possible.

N.B. For the **canasta tango**, the couple change sides (reverse Kilian). The boy takes the place of the girl and vice versa.

The Kilian hold

Open hold or hand-in-hand

This is a hold where both parties skate forward, each holding by only one arm. The joining arm is held out almost straight, with the girl (usually) slightly in front of the boy.

Open hold can also be used when skating backwards.

The open hold

Waltz hold

During this hold both parties skate with their shoulders facing each other. The boy's right hand is placed on his partner's back (by the shoulder blade). The girl's left arm rests on the boy's right arm. The girl's right arm joins the boy's left. See photo.

Now let's take a look at the **Dutch waltz**.

The waltz hold

Dutch waltz

The Dutch Waltz is a superb introductory ice dance. Only forward skating is used (along with the Kilian hold), together with a few runs/progressives, a couple of swing rolls and good basic forward stroking. As the name implies, this is skated to a waltz tempo and on almost every ice rink session there will be an opportunity for you to try out this dance, with or without a partner.

Start out by pushing on to an outside edge on your left foot, followed by a cross on to an inside on the right. There is then a forward run/progressive to the left, an outside edge and two swing rolls, firstly to the right, then to the left.

Run/progressive to the right, outside edge, then bring the feet together and push on to an outside on the left foot, followed by an inside on the right. Finish with a run/progressive to the left, followed with a swing roll to the right. Repeat the sequence.

All compulsory dances have a set pattern that must be strictly followed. Look at the diagram below and you will see a plan of the Dutch waltz as it would look if you were a fly on the ceiling of the rink.

N.B. Don't be put off by the various groups of letters used to describe each step. If you see RFO, all this describes is a right foot forward outside edge. The first letter tells you the foot on which you should be standing, the second letter refers to the direction, and the third, which edge to use, outside or inside. Should you see additional words such as swing roll, this again speaks for itself.

The time interval for which you must hold each step is marked on the pattern.

N.B. Dutch waltz was invented by George Muller. It was first skated at the Broadmoor Ice Palace, Colorado Springs in 1948.

Music — waltz 3/4

Tempo — 46 measures of 3 beats — 138 beats per minute

DUTCH WALTZ / SET PATTERN DANCE

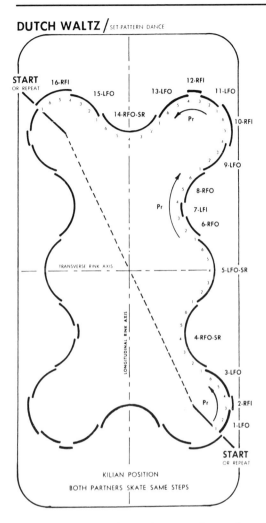

Another good introductory dance is called the **preliminary foxtrot**.

Preliminary foxtrot

This dance is skated in Kilian hold. There are usually four introductory steps (left, right, left, right, all on outside edges), followed by a forward run/progressive (2 steps) and an outside swing roll. This is followed by exactly the same sequence, but on the other foot in the other direction.

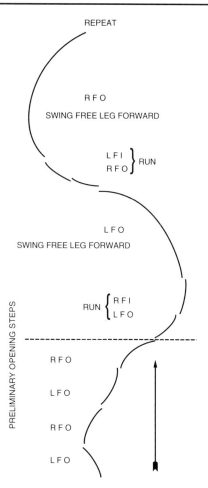

REPEAT

RFO
SWING FREE LEG FORWARD

LFI
RFO } RUN

LFO
SWING FREE LEG FORWARD

RUN { RFI
LFO

PRELIMINARY OPENING STEPS

RFO

LFO

RFO

LFO

Music and tempo — foxtrot 4/4
LFO — 1 count
RFO — 1 count
LFO swing — 4 counts

Canasta tango

The canasta tango is yet another superb introductory dance. The girl remains on the inside of the guy throughout.

Both parties skate the same steps.

Push on to a forward outside left edge, followed by a forward outside right then a forward run/progressive to the left. There is then a left foot forward chasse, followed by a swing roll on the left foot. The feet are brought back together, followed by a slide chasse on the right foot.

There is then a swing roll on the right foot, followed by a slide chasse on the left foot, followed by a left foot run/progressive and a cross roll on to the right foot. The steps are then repeated, starting from the forward run/progressive to the left.

CANASTA TANGO/ SET PATTERN DANCE

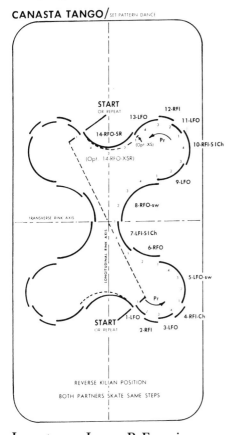

Inventor — James B Francis
First performed — University Skating Club, Toronto (1951)
Music — Tango 4/4
Tempo — 26 measures of 4 beats — 104 per minute

How can I find a partner?

There are always plenty of people looking for skating partners.

If you want to progress reasonably it is important to find someone of your standard or perhaps a little better. It is great fun learning the dances together, but it helps a great deal if one or the other already has a good idea of what is meant to be happening.

Before deciding on your partner you should ask the opinion of a professional coach as to how well you blend both physically and in standard.

To be able to take part in any tests or competitions you must have somebody to skate with so the sooner you find that person the better.

If you are unable to find a suitable partner in the rink, you can always advertise in the skating magazine, stating your age group, height and standard.

SUMMARY

This chapter covers the basic requirements of ice dancing. Ice dancing amounts to performing various moves and sequences of footwork to music with a set rhythm. In championship ice dancing, there are three sections: 1 the compulsory dances, which consist of set step sequences fitted to music of a particular character, which are repeated; 2 the original rhythm dance, which is a dance made up by the skaters to fit a particular character and musical tempo, which can last up to two minutes and ten seconds; 3 the free dance, which is a programme of either three or four minutes in length, devised by the skaters to show off their originality.

The next section deals with some basic dance steps. A forward chasse involves starting on one foot on an outside edge, and changing feet, raising up the free leg slightly and standing on an inside edge, followed by a third push which is the same as the first one.

A forward run or progressive involves a series of steps running either clockwise or anticlockwise. The first step is usually on to an outside edge and the second an inside edge.

A slide chasse amounts to a push on to an outside edge, followed by a change of foot on to an inside edge, sliding the free foot off the ice and holding it in front of the skating foot.

A swing roll involves pushing on to an outside edge on one foot and stretching the free leg back and then swinging that leg in front of the skating foot.

A cross roll and swing amounts to crossing one foot over the other, changing feet and a swing roll.

The next section covers the Dutch waltz, which is a good introductory dance, involving forward stroking, progressives and swing rolls, all performed to a waltz tempo.

The preliminary foxtrot consists of a forward progressive run, followed by an outside swing roll, repeatedly skated to the left and the right.

The canasta tango is a simple dance using only forward skating.

There are diagrams of each dance with the steps coded in the following fashion. The first letter denotes the foot, the second the direction and the third the edge you should be using.

14 *Pair Skating*

There are few sporting activities that compare with the exciting and daring elements contained within a championship pair-skating routine.

In recent times pair skating has developed in many different and dramatic ways and even in its most basic form it is one of the most attractive areas of the sport.

Pair skating combines tremendous athleticism with great artistry and entertainment, and as such is one area which shows off many of the most difficult and spectacular ice-skating moves.

Championship pair skating should be witnessed live to do it justice, as many speed effects are lost on television. How can you fit an Olympic ice rink onto a 25in. screen, without paying some kind of price?

Pair skating includes input from all the other areas of figure skating. From the compulsory figures come the strong edges and changes of position, whereas ice dancing contributes the uniformity required to make two skaters appear to move as one. The great triple jumps and complicated spins come from free skating.

But pair skating does have many original moves. There are the huge overhead lifts, some involving the girl being held over her partner's head by only one hand. Then there are the throws. This is when the man assists the girl into huge multi-rotational jumps, that she must land by herself. Such moves as the throw double axel gain great height and travel enormous distances, requiring much strength and skill from both parties.

Last but not least there are the death spirals where the girl is held by her partner in such a position that her head is almost touching the ice.

The death spiral, demonstrated by the 1990 Junior British Pairs Champions, Vicky Pearce and Clive Shorten

Basic requirements

If you feel particularly drawn to pair skating, there are a few facts that you should consider first.

The boy has to be able to lift and throw his partner without any obvious difficulties. He must be physically strong, as must his partner.

If you are not and wish to become a competent pair skater, you should go to your local sports centre and learn how to use weights along with cycling, running and anything else that you are advised to do by a fitness expert.

How to choose a partner

When it comes to looking for a partner, there are several considerations that must be met. Firstly, it is usual for the girl to be both lighter and smaller than her partner. If this is not the case, the pair will look rather odd and most probably will have great difficulty in learning even the most basic moves (unless the girl lifts and throws the boy).

Secondly, the couple should blend physically. This means that both parties should have similar builds. For example, if the girl has a slim build it would be aesthetically pleasing if her partner has the same. Thirdly, both skaters should be of a similar standard. This means that they are both able to perform jumps and spins at about the same level.

N.B. The individual moves incorporated within any routine must be reliable. There is no advantage in one person being able to do a jump if the other has great problems doing the same.

How do I start?

Before starting out in this area, you would be well advised to make your own forward and backward skating as good as possible, working on your posture and speed.

Now find somebody who fits the criteria covered in the previous section and practise skating together, forwards and backwards in both Kilian and open hold. (See Chapter 13.)

Before trying anything difficult, it is a good idea to try to skate a couple of simple dances together, such as the Dutch waltz and preliminary foxtrot. (See Chapter 13.)

Try skating forwards in both directions, clockwise and counter-clockwise. If you are using an open hold (when you are holding each other by one hand only), do make sure that when skating forward the girl is slightly in front. The joining arm should be held pretty straight.

When skating backwards in open hold, the man generally leads, again the joining arm should be held firmly.

When skating either backwards or forwards, make sure that you and your partner bend and push at the same time and, whatever else you do, keep in step — as nothing looks worse than seeing one person out of sync with the other!

Check that your free legs are equally stretched and in line. When skating forward, the girl should be slightly in front of the boy and as you both become more comfortable, work on increasing your speed and free leg extension.

You should now try some backwards skating. The boy should lead on backward crossovers (crosscuts). Hold on to each other using only one hand. If you are skating anticlockwise, the man's left hand should be holding the girl's right. If you are skating clockwise, the arms should be reversed, so that the join is between the man's right and the girl's left.

The arms linking each other must be straight and the girl should ensure that she stays in line, following on the same circle as her partner. Hold your free arms so there is a line from the boy's free hand down to the girl's. Practise this move in both directions.

If you wish to go ahead in this direction, you should now seriously consider hiring some professional help.

Famous pair skaters

The top pair skaters of the 1990s now complete effortless side by side triple jumps and are simply amazing.

Rodnina and Zaitsev, probably the most famous pair skaters of all time

Much of the progress in this discipline is due to the Soviets, who have dominated the sport for many years, partly as a result of being great innovators.

Probably the greatest pair skater ever is Irina Rodnina, who with two different partners, Alexei Ulanov and then Alexander Zaitsev, won so many world titles along with three Olympic Gold Medals.

One of the few exceptional non-Soviet couples was Barbara Underhill and Paul Martini, who won the 1984 Gold Medal for Canada, along with Tai Babilonia and Randy Gardner of the United States, who won the 1979 World Championship.

SUMMARY

Pair skating is one of the most difficult, physically demanding yet most stunning disciplines in the sport.

Great physical strength is needed by both parties, to undertake the lifts, throws, and general free skating requirements of pair skating.

A good physical match is desirable. This means that the girl must be smaller and lighter than the man, and with the same type of build. If one is slim, so the other must be too.

If you decide to try out with a partner, start by practising forwards and backwards skating in various dance-type holds. You must keep in step at all times and your body positions must match. Any solo free-skating moves attempted side by side must be reliable and your entries and exits must be exactly timed.

If you find a potential partner, employ a good professional coach to teach you the various moves.

15 *Precision Skating*

There is now a relatively new area of ice skating in which people of all age groups and levels of skating competence can take part and compete.

This discipline is called precision skating and it amounts to groups of skaters performing steps and various group formations to music.

To set the scene, precision skating started up in the late 1970s in Canada and by the mid 1980s the Canadians were holding national championships.

As a result of this enthusiasm, the interest in precision skating was exported to other countries, and in 1990 the International Skating Union accepted and recognized the area as one of the official disciplines, along with figure skating, ice dancing, pair skating and speed.

Precision skating is currently one of the fastest-growing areas of the sport.

The Ice Jemettes, The Lee Valley Novice Precision Team

One of the first considerations is to ensure the accuracy of the skating and of the various block moves; in fact the main point of it all is for each team to move as one entity.

Basic rules

The teams may consist of girls, boys, or a combination of both, and may include up to a maximum of six substitutes.

There are specific categories, based on age groups, into which teams must fit. Any team from a particular category will skate against other teams of the same category.

Currently, there are five. These are as follows:

1. **Juvenile** Team of between twelve and thirty-two members. The skaters must be under the age of twelve on the 1st January preceding the competition. The programme length is three minutes.

2. **Novice** Team of between twelve and thirty-two members, aged under fourteen on the 1st January preceding the competition. The programme length is three and a half minutes.

3. **Junior** Team of between twelve and twenty skaters with no age limit. The programme length is four minutes.

The Ice Jems.
The Lee
Valley Junior
Precision
Team, 1990

4. **Senior** Team of between twenty-one and thirty skaters, with no age limit. The programme length is four and a half minutes.

5. **Adult** Team of between twelve and thirty skaters. The skaters must be over the age of twenty-one on the 1st January preceding the competition, with 75 per cent of the team over the age of twenty-five. The programme length is three and a half minutes.

The music used must consist of three distinct rhythms of at least two differing tempos. The music can include vocals. (It should be said that vocals are not permitted in any other area of non professional competition.)

The music must be appropriate for the age group of the skater. For example, adults would probably look rather silly skating to childlike music and a very young team might not suit an adult theme.

The costumes should be designed to perform to distinct functions. Firstly they must be a visual aid to musical interpretation. Secondly, they should be as flattering as possible to the wearers.

All U.K. skaters who wish to take part must be members of the National Skating Association, (address in the appendix).

As long as you are of a reasonable skating standard, you will be able to find a team to join, and if not, get together with some friends and form your own.

16 *Canskate Programme And N.S.A. Award Scheme*

The Canadian Figure Skating Association has devised an excellent skating programme which they have specially designed to encourage new skaters to develop their skating skills.

Participants are constantly evaluated until they are able to take the proficiency test. The result has been to create an interesting and fun environment by combining warm-up exercises, group instruction, ice games and warm-down exercises with music. The result has been great motivation and increased enthusiasm for the sport.

CANSKATE consists of eight badges and they are as follows:

1 **Beginner**
2 **Elementary**
3 **Basic**
4 **Novice I**
5 **Novice II**
6 **Novice III**
7 **Novice IV**
8 **Proficiency Test**

Objectives of the Canskate Programme

The objectives of the CANSKATE Programme are to provide an enjoyable, safe skating programme; to develop balance, coordination and rhythm through the use of music; to teach correct technique for forward skating, backward skating, stopping, turning, spinning, jumping along with the four basic edges. This programme aims to provide incentives for beginners, to promote physical fitness and to encourage lifelong participation in the sport, along with motivating the skaters to learn figure skating.

Who teaches and evaluates the Canskate Programme?

The CANSKATE Programme may be taught by professional or amateur coaches who have been certified at a C.F.S.A. CANSKATE COACHES' CLINIC. The coaches also evaluate the progress of the skaters on a day to day basis. Badges are awarded once skaters have demonstrated the ability to perform all of the required elements and they have achieved their Desired Performance Level. The Proficiency Test is the only badge in the CANSKATE Programme that requires formal testing. The Proficiency Test can be judged by:

1 A Professional coach
2 A CANFIGURESKATE coach
3 A CANSKATE coach

How long does it take to complete?

This is a difficult question to answer because many factors determine a skater's rate of progress. The amount of ice time available, equipment, age, ability and quality of instruction affect a skater's progress. On the average, skaters will complete the programme in two seasons. However, some skaters will require less time to complete the programme whilst others such as pre-school children will take a little longer.

Can the badges be taken in any order?

Badges should be completed in order, as the programme is designed to follow a natural teaching progression. If a skater is delayed in acquiring a badge due to inability to perform one or two elements, he or she should start working at the next badge level, and continue to practise the missed elements of the previous badge. When these elements are mastered, the badge will be issued.

What comes after the Canskate Programme?

CANSKATE is the starting point for all skaters. Once through the CANSKATE Programme, skaters and parents should be advised of the various options available. If a skater shows the desire and necessary ability and providing the financial resources are available, the skater should be encouraged to enter the C.F.S.A. Test stream. If interest, ability and resources are moderate the next logical option is to enter the CANFIGURESKATE Programme, which is primarily a recreational figure-skating programme.

Where can I enrol?

The CANSKATE Programme is offered by member clubs of the Canadian Figure Skating Association and by community recreation organizations.

Programme outline

The CANSKATE Programme is a learn-to-skate programme for beginners of all ages. Forward skating, backward skating, stopping, turning, spinning, jumping and the four basic edges are taught in the CANSKATE Programme.

There is no formal testing in the CANSKATE Programme except for the Proficiency Test. CANSKATE skills are assessed by the coach on a day-to-day basis and a badge is awarded when all of the skills can be performed at the Desired Performance Level. The Proficiency Test can be judged by a professional coach, a CANFIGURESKATE coach or a CANSKATE coach.

Beginner badge

1 Sitting down and getting up
2 Balance and posture
3 Left push off/right forward glide for three counts
4 Right push off/left forward glide for three counts
5 Falling down
6 Two-foot jumping on the spot
7 Turning on the spot (clockwise and counterclockwise)
8 Step sequence with one count per step (minimum of six steps)
9 Half snow plough stop (LFI)
10 Half snow plough stop (RFI)
11 Forward skating across the width of the rink (alternate feet)
12 Upright two-foot glide into half sitting glide
13 Backward two-foot skating (L/R/L/R or R/L/R/L)

Note: A Pre-Beginner Badge may be awarded to skaters who do not qualify for the Beginner Badge at the end of the season.

Elementary badge

1 Two-foot spin (minimum of two rotations)
2 Left push-off/right forward glide for four counts/left stop
3 Right push-off/left forward glide for four counts/right stop
4 Forward two-foot glide on a curve
5 Forward one-foot glide on a curve
6 Backward two-foot skating (eight consecutive push-glide sequences)
7 Two-foot turn — forwards to backwards
8 Two-foot turn — backwards to forwards
9 Forward stroking across the width of the rink (two counts per glide)/half snowplough stop
10 Slalom (forwards in any manner)

Basic badge

1 Forward bunny hop − left or right
2 Forward circle thrusts − clockwise
3 Forward crosscuts − (minimum of six consecutive)
4 Forward circle thrusts − counterclockwise
5 Forward crosscuts − counterclockwise (minimum of six consecutive)
6 Two-foot jump − forwards to backwards
7 LFO-LBI three turn
8 RFO-RBI three turn
9 Forward stroking across the width of the rink (four counts per glide)/half snowplough stop
10 Backward two-foot skating across the width of the rink (alternate push/glide sequences)

Novice I Badge

1 Forward spiral in a straight line − left foot
2 Forward spiral in a straight line − right foot
3 Backward one-foot glide (four counts per glide on alternate feet, minimum of four push-glide sequences)
4 Backward half snowplough stop (LBI)
5 Backward half snowplough stop (RBI)
6 Two-foot jump − backwards to forwards
7 LBI-RFI Mohawk
8 RBI-LFI Mohawk
9 Forward outside edge

Novice II Badge

1 Backward circle thrusts with RBO glide for two counts (counterclockwise)
2 Backward crosscuts − counterclockwise (minimum of six consecutive)
3 Backward circle thrusts with LBO glide for two counts − clockwise
4 Backward crosscuts − clockwise (minimum of six consecutive)
5 LBO-RFO Mohawk
6 RBO-LFO Mohawk

7 Waltz jump
8 Forward inside edges
9 Slalom (edges or crosscuts, forwards and/or backwards)

Novice III Badge

1 LFO-LBI three jump
2 RFO-RBI three jump
3 Forward two-foot parallel side stop — to the left
4 Forward two-foot parallel side stop — to the right
5 Backward circle thrusts with RBO glide for four counts — counterclockwise
6 Backward circle thrusts with LBO glide for four counts — clockwise
7 Backward outside edges
8 Forward crosscuts/LFO-LBI three turn/backward crosscuts/RBO-LFO Mohawk on counterclockwise circle. Repeat a minimum of three times
9 Forward crosscuts/RFO-RBI three turn/backward crosscuts/LBO-RFO Mohawk on clockwise circle. Repeat a minimum of three times
10 LFI-RBI Mohawk
11 Forward crosscuts/LFI-RBI Mohawk/backward crosscuts/RBI-LFI Mohawk on a clockwise circle. Repeat a minimum of three times
12 RFI-LBI Mohawk
13 Forward crosscuts/RBI-LBI Mohawk/backward crosscuts/LBI-RFI Mohawk on a counterclockwise circle. Repeat a minimum of four times

Novice IV Badge

1 Backward inside edges
2 LFO-LBI three turn/RBO edge on a counterclockwise circle. Repeat a minimum of four times
3 RFO-RBI three turn/LBO edge on a counterclockwise circle. Repeat a minimum of four times
4 LFI-LBO three turn
5 RFI-RBO three turn
6 LFI-LBO three jump

7 RFI-RBO three jump
8 Forward crosscuts in a figure 8 pattern
9 Backward crosscuts in a figure 8 pattern

Proficiency test

The Proficiency Test must be judged by:
A professional coach familiar with the programme
A certified CANFIGURESKATE coach
A certified CANSKATE coach
It is recommended that a professional coach judge the Proficiency Test whenever possible

1 Forward outside edges
2 Forward inside edges
3 Backward outside edges
4 Backward inside edges
5 Forward stroking two laps (crosscuts at the ends) RFO-RBI three turn or LFI-RBI Mohawk/ backward stroking two laps (crosscuts at the ends) − clockwise
6 Forward stroking two laps (crosscuts at the ends) LFO-LBI three turn or RFI-LBI Mohawk/ backward stroking two laps (crosscuts at the ends) − counterclockwise

For more information please contact the Canadian Figure Skating Association, 1600 James Naismith Drive, Gloucester, Ontario K1B 5N4.
[This section has been reproduced with permission of Barbara Wilson, Pr Assistant, C.F.S.A..]

National Skating Association of Great Britain award scheme

The National Skating Association has formulated a series of skating tests designed to encourage the developing skaters early on in their careers.

These 'Star Awards' can be taken during any skating session when there is an approved judge at hand.

They cover the various manoeuvres learned by all new skaters, starting from forward skating and developing through the edges and turns essential to skating progress. This is also the operational system in most British ice rinks.

These awards are ideal for young children who can try the test and buy the badge on successful completion, along with a certificate when they have acquired the whole series.

For the purposes of this book, I plan to cover only the first eight 'Star Awards', and it should be said that most of the moves described are all contained within the preceding teaching chapters. So if you want to check out exactly what is required for each level, locate the relevant award and follow this up by looking at the mentioned elements in the particular section of the book.

For those of you who wish to advance beyond this level, there are advanced awards applicable to all areas of the sport, and the ice-dance section alone consists of thirty.

N.S.A. Star Awards

1a) Skate forward across the rink without falling over.
 b) Sit on the ice and get up unaided in a safe manner.

2a) Skate forward on alternate feet, showing some understanding of the use of the blade, to the centre of the rink and stop, using any recognized method.
 b) Skate backwards across the rink without pausing or falling over.
 c) Skate forward on one foot for a count of at least three seconds, using both the left and the right foot.

3a) Skate forward on alternate feet, minimum of five steps, then glide on two feet into a sitting position holding on to the boots with both hands for a count of three seconds. Mature skaters need only achieve a partial sitting.

b) Three or more optional forward steps finishing on a forward outside edge, with the free foot extended behind for a count of at least three seconds, using one foot then the other.

c) Skate backwards on alternate feet showing some understanding of the free foot position.

4a) Skate forward to the centre of the rink without stopping, any turn, and continue to skate backwards in the same direction into a backwards stop.

b) Three or more optional backward steps finishing on a backward outside edge with the free foot extended for a count of at least three seconds, left and right foot.

c) Step from a backward glide to a forward glide, left and right foot.

5a) Consecutive forward outside edges on alternate feet showing some understanding of the hip and shoulder positions. Each edge must be at least one third of a circle.

b) Continuous forward open chasses on a circle, clockwise and counterclockwise. Following each step the free leg must be lifted clear of the ice.

c) Forward outside three turn, left and right foot. The edges before and after the turn must be reasonably controlled and moderate in length.

6a) Consecutive forward inside edges on alternate feet showing some understanding of hip and shoulder positions. Each edge must be at least one third of a circle in length.

b) Continuous backward outside edges. Each edge must be at least one third of a circle in length.

c) Continuous backward open chasses on a circle, clockwise and counterclockwise. The skating foot must lift off the ice on the end of each step.

7a) Continuous forward runs on a circle, left and right foot.

b) Continuous backward crossovers on a circle, clockwise and counterclockwise.

c) Forward inside closed Mohawk showing correct position of the free foot after the turn. Both feet must be completed.

8a) Forward closed chasses on alternate feet, (LFO, X chasse RFI, LFO, RFO, X chasse, LFI, RFO).

b) Change of edge forward outside to inside, left and right. Each edge must be moderate in length. The arms and free leg should be used to assist in the movement.

c) Forward inside open Mohawk showing the correct position of the free leg after the turn. This is to be performed on alternate feet.

It should be said that in order to take these tests the skater must be a registered National Skating Association skater and this address can be found in the appendix, so if you would like some information, you would be well advised to get in touch with the association directly.

They will supply you with a membership card which you should bring along. To be awarded the test, all sections must be successfully completed, at the same time and the Personal Achievement Chart supplied to each candidate must be retained and presented to the judge on the occasion of each test. On successful completion of the test, the skater is entitled to buy the relevant test badge.

17 *How is Ice Skating Judged?*

The way ice skating is judged is probably not as complex as many people imagine.

For any competition there is an odd number of judges, so that there can always be room for a dissenting view along with a majority decision.

This means that there may be three, five, seven or nine judges on a competition panel. On tests this is not necessarily so. On some tests only two judges are required and in others three. In some countries a single panel senior judge is sufficient.

When watching the performers, the judges will be looking for specific points and these will vary according to the discipline being marked. I feel that the best way to explain this is to cover each area of the sport and point out the most relevant points that the judges will be looking for.

What the judges look for in ice dancing

Compulsory dances

In ice dancing, there are several important criteria that the skaters should fill.

First, skating in time with the music. Every step that forms part of a compulsory dance has a specified time period (as well as edge, pattern, etc.) allotted to it. To gain high marks this requirement must be fulfilled to the satisfaction of the judges. In fact many judges take the view that if a skater is not in time with the music, he is not dancing and therefore few marks can be awarded for the effort.

The second area of great importance is that of unison. This means that the skaters must move as one. Their free legs must have equal extension, their pushes must be absolutely as one and every move should appear as effortless as possible. They must have good posture.

Strong edges are considered important and these are generally represented by strong curves. There must be good musical interpretation which can be explained by saying that if the skaters are dancing a tango, there must be no doubt that their moves reflect the character of a tango.

There is a single mark out of six for each dance.

Original-rhythm dance

When judging the original-rhythm dance, the judges look for other things in addition to those mentioned above.

Firstly, it is important to be aware of what is required of an original rhythm dance. Basically, this is a dance routine choreographed by or for the skaters, which interprets a particular character and tempo. This is set for the subsequent year so that the skaters have time to get their act (and their routine) together.

The judges will see the skaters perform a dance which is two minutes in length and may contain a maximum of two pieces of music. This will give them the opportunity to judge such areas as timing, originality, technical difficulty, and good use of the ice along with strong edges.

Marks for this routine are awarded out of six for technical merit and artistic impression.

The last area that the panel must judge is the free dance.

Free dance

Isabelle and Paul Duchesnay, highly original World Ice Dance Champions, 1991

The free dance is the couple's opportunity to show the judges their originality and technical capabilities within the allotted time (usually four minutes). The judges will mark the couple on the basis of their speed, unison, use of the ice, along with their style and interpretative capabilities.

There are two marks awarded. The first is for technical merit and the second is for artistic impression.

How compulsory figures are judged

The compulsory figures are given marks in accordance with the geometrical accuracy of the circles and their alignment with each other. The diameter should be equivalent to between two and a half and three times the skater's height.

Should the figures involve turns, accurate placement and cleanness of turn is required along with style, carriage, flow and running edge.

How free skating is judged

Free skating is judged in a slightly different way from ice dancing. The quality of skating edges, style, soft movement over the ice along with carriage, flow and utilisation of the available space are observed. There is no pre-set mark. Marks are assessed at the end of the performance when jumps, spins, steps, etc. are compared to previous skaters and the marks are then determined.

Championship free skating consists of programmes of a certain pre-selected length. The first programme is called the original free programme.

Original free programme

The original free programme is a routine or programme devised by or for each skater in the championship. The programme must not be longer than two minutes and forty seconds.

The programme will contain certain pre-selected movements that all the skaters must complete. This usually consists of particular jumps and jump combinations, spins and jump spins. The combination jump occurs where one jump is a prescribed move and the other is a free choice. Naturally enough, a more difficult second jump will earn higher marks than an easier one; however, a good quality double jump is better than a poor quality triple.

If a prescribed jump is a double axel this must be performed; if a skater jumps a triple marks will be deducted for not doing the prescribed move.

There are also set step sequences that must form a particular pattern over the ice. There are also certain spins and combinations of spins, with a specified minimum number of rotations that must be completed.

All these moves must be completed in the time allowed and, at the same time, interpret whatever music the skater is using.

Each judge will allocate two marks, like ice dancing out of a maximum of six. The first mark will be for technical or content difficulty and the second will be for artistic impression, or the style and carriage along with the interpretation of the music used.

Kristi Yamaguchi, USA. A great stylist and 1991 World Champion

The other part of the free-skating competition deals with the long free-skating programme.

The long free programme

In international competitions this is now four and a half minutes for men and four minutes for women. This programme has no set elements, but is the skaters' opportunity to show the judges all of their great skills. It should contain the jumps, spins and choreography of the greatest ingenuity and technical difficulty. The judges will award marks on the basis of such things as the technical content and the style and sureness of the moves that are included. A fall for example will inevitably cause a loss of marks for several reasons: the break in the continuity, the loss of time and the fact that the move has failed.

Kurt Browning, Canada's 1991 World Champion

149

The only restrictions in the long free are as follows:

A triple jump can only be repeated in combinations or during jump sequences, thus eliminating a skater including ten to twelve triple Salchows which is both repetitive and boring.

Pair skating

As with the free-skating programmes mentioned above, pair skating consists of a compulsory along with a long free-skating programme.

Dynamic Canadian pair skaters, Isabelle Brasseur and Lloyd Eisler

Original programme

The original programme will have certain specified moves, including lifts, pair spins, solo jumps and spins along with step sequences. There are no throws in the original programme!

Marks are awarded for both technical merit and artistic impression in accordance with the moves performed along with the manner of performance. There is a major additional factor that the judges must consider: along with the completion of all these moves, the unison of the couple must take a high priority in their decision-making.

The other section is the long programme which, like the free skating is the pair skaters' opportunity to show all their technical and artistic brilliance to the judges.

Precision skating

Precision skating is marked on the basis of two specific areas.

The first covers **composition**, which amounts to originality, technical difficulty, placement of the manoeuvres on the ice, cleanness and sureness, continuous skating on edges with speed and flow along with smooth precise transitions.

The second mark is for **presentation** and covers unison and musical synchronization, carriage and style, the variety of music and movements in rhythm with the music, the correct selection of music relating to the age and ability of the team and finally the harmonious compositon of the programme as a whole and its conformity to the music chosen.

What happens to the marks?

There is one area of the marking system which may cause a few problems. Although the total number of marks awarded may be a significant figure, this does not necessarily have a bearing on the results.

The results are based on a system of placements. If you are placed second by one judge, he will have given you two place marks. Should another judge place you third, she will have given you three place marks.

The total number of place marks awarded by all the judges are added together for each skater. These are then compared to those given to all the other skaters and the resulting final places are calculated.

This means that if the majority of judges have placed a skater in first place, this is where the skater will end up, and if the majority have placed somebody second, that is where that skater will finish.

The scoring system ensures that an over-enthusiastic judge cannot give a high mark that can influence the final positions and vice versa.

Therefore the final placings amount to the total number of placements gained by the skater. The winner will have the least number and the person placed last will have the highest number.

SUMMARY

This chapter covers the apparently mystical ice skating marking system.

The first section area relates to what the judges look for when marking different sections of each skating discipline.

The last section deals with how the competitors are awarded their final places.

18 *Speed Skating*

Most people associate speed skating with the Dutch people and there are in fact some extremely good reasons for this. Speed skating started during the thirteenth century on the canals of Holland. The races came later, the major developments being made in the eighteenth and nineteenth centuries.

The early races took place on straight tracks, but, in the course of the nineteenth century, these were replaced by U-shaped tracks. In those days, the races usually involved two people racing against each other.

Speed skating was brought over to the United Kingdom by the Frieslanders and naturally enough the area of the country that they used for the races was similar to Holland, namely the fen country near Cambridge.

Indoor or short-track speed skating began in the 1920s, the first British club being formed at Richmond Ice Rink. This club was soon followed by a series of others throughout the country.

After the International Skating Union was formed, the first World Championships were held.

Modern speed skaters do not have quite the same problems finding somewhere to skate as did their ancestors. However, there are very few long course or 400-metre oval tracks on which to train and currently none in the United Kingdom.

This fact led to the setting up of the two forms of speed skating that we have today. These are firstly, the long course as mentioned above and the short course, which uses a 111.12 metre track. Short course can be undertaken in the majority of the rinks in the U.K.

Such is the popularity of speed skating that most of the British rinks have speed-skating clubs and overall participation in the sport has increased enormously in the last few years.

Speed skaters are the fastest-moving self-propelled sports people over level ground. Downhill skiers will certainly achieve more speed, but they do have considerable help from gravity.

Short-track speed skating takes place at indoor ice rinks and the season runs from September to May.

The system of racing used in short track is different from that used for outdoor speed and this difference lies in the fact that short track races are run between *Wilf* various competitors, whereas outdoor speed races are *O'Reilly,* solely against the clock.

Britain's Short-track speed skating is to become an Olympic *world-class* event from 1992, having been recognized as an official *short-track* International Skating Union World Championship *speed skater* event since 1982.

Club events are held each season from September until May, and these events take place at weekends and move from one speed club to the next throughout the season.

Speed-skating equipment

The type of equipment used by speed skaters is quite different from that used by figure or hockey skaters.

The boots have much lower internal supports and the blade is considerably longer and thinner to allow minimum friction between itself and the ice and therefore maximum speed.

Outdoor speed skates are longer and have flat blades. The pillars which carry the blades are lower too. In short track, the boots are made partly from fibre glass and partly from leather, the blades are shorter and not flat. This is to ensure some grip when cornering on small rinks, and the supporting pillars are higher.

The outfits worn by the skaters do not vary as for both outdoor and short track races the competitors wear tight fitting lycra suits.

It is compulsory for all short track racers to wear hard shell helmets and gloves, whereas outdoor racers are not compelled to wear either. Some skaters wear knee and elbow pads.

Safety pads are placed over the barriers to minimize any risk of injury due to collision.

The track

The 111.12 oval track used in short track speed skating fits neatly on to an Olympic size ice rink. Small 3-inch square wooden or dome-shaped rubber blocks are placed around the curves of the track. These blocks mark the corners of the track and the skaters must keep to the outside of them.

As you might imagine, the track is marked according to the distances and number of competitors, in fact on a large rink there can be up to five tracks.

In outdoor speed events there are two lanes with the requirement that each skater make a cross over from one track to the other on each circuit to ensure that each skates exactly the same distance. Only two skaters race at any one time.

Race distances

Competitions are run over several distances depending upon the rules laid down by the organization running the event. In the United Kingdom they are as follows: 222 metres (2 laps), 333 metres (3 laps), 400 metres (3 laps), 500 metres (4 laps).

800 metres (7 laps), 1000 metres (9 laps), 1500 metres (13 laps), 3000 metres (27 laps).

The shorter 222 and 333 metres are skated only by junior skaters.

Relay races — 3000 metres (27 laps), 5000 metres (45 laps).

There are also various categories according to age and they are as follows:

> Senior Men/Senior Ladies
> Juniors (under 16 years of age)
> Juveniles (under 14 years of age)
> Pee Wees (under 12 years of age)

Speed skating is organized in the United Kingdom by the National Skating Association, whose address is in the appendix at the back of the book. Should you require more information, contact the N.S.A.

19 *Ice Hockey*

Ice hockey is the second most popular sport in the world. The name may well be derived from the French word, 'hoquet', which means a shepherd's crook, and this just so happens to be the approximate shape of an ice-hockey stick.

There are several theories as to how ice hockey originated, varying from a game played by North American Indians in the eighteenth century to that played by British soldiers stationed in Canada in the nineteenth.

Although the game was most probably exported to Canada from the north of England, it is undoubtedly true that the first set of rules were compiled by a certain Mr Creighton, who was a student at McGill University, Montreal.

Some students from McGill University formed the first team in 1879 and from that point onwards the game rapidly spread across Canada and the United States. The first World Championship was held in Montreal in 1883, during the Ice Carnival and naturally enough was won by the team from McGill University. In 1886, the Amateur Hockey Association of Canada was formed, consisting of representatives from Montreal, Quebec and Ottawa.

In 1893, the Governor General of the time, Lord Stanley of Preston, donated a cup named after him. This 'Stanley Cup', first played for in March 1894, is still the most sought-after reward in the game.

The first ice hockey matches were played in rather basic circumstances, on outdoor ice surfaces, using wooden goal posts along with snow banks to mark the edges of the playing area, or the barriers/boards to us. (In those days, the teams consisted of nine players on each side, and forward passing was not permitted.)

Many of the rules were adopted from rugby and field hockey. Inevitably the possibility of a few scuffles and fights attracted many of the early supporters.

Soon after the turn of the century, ice hockey began to catch on in Europe with the resulting formation of the International Ice Hockey Federation in 1908 at a meeting in Vienna. The founder members of this organization were the United Kingdom, France, Switzerland, Belgium and Bohemia, followed by Germany in 1909.

The first International Championships in the game were held during the Antwerp Winter Olympic Games of 1920. The winners were the Winnipeg Falcons.

In the United Kingdom, there has always been considerable Canadian involvement, with many of the teams having at least a few dual-national Canadian/British players.

Under the influence of the professional leagues, the sport began to take on its current form, with such developments as six players on each side, and the introduction of three twenty-minute periods, and, in the early 1930s, the right for players to forward pass.

In 1917 the National Hockey League of North America (N.H.L.) was formed. Since 1943 the N.H.L. has amounted to a great competition between the Boston Bruins, the Chicago Blackhawks, the Detroit Red Wings, the Montreal Canadiens, the New York Rangers and the Toronto Maple Leafs. Since that time some more clubs have been added.

In the United Kingdom there was a great deal of interest in the sport along with some spectacular successes culminating in the gold medal at the 1936 Olympic Games. At this time there was a great deal of growth in the number of ice rinks available and the interest in skating generally reflected this fact.

Unfortunately, due to several factors including the Second World War and the lack of seating in ice rinks, the sport faded out for a while. There was another revival after the war but no major developments took place until recent times.

That was during the last ten years. There has been a great renewal of interest and, fortunately, many new rinks built that can seat sufficient people to make hockey matches economically viable. The sport has received a great deal of sponsorship from all areas of commerce and there is a fair amount of television coverage. With all of this interest, the future of ice hockey looks secure.

Ice hockey equipment

In a game of ice hockey there are two teams each consisting of six players. They use wooden sticks limited to 147 centimetres in length with a 32-centimetre blade. The goalkeeper is permitted to use a slightly heavier and wider blade. This instrument is used to hit a puck which is made from vulcanized rubber, 7.62 centimetres in diameter, 2.52 centimetres in width and weighing not less than 156 and not more than 170 grammes.

An Olympic ice hockey match between USSR and Poland

The players wear a great deal of protective clothing. This includes such items as knee and elbow pads, shoulder and shin guards, great gloves, long socks that cover the knee pads along with shorts and sweaters in the relevant team colours. The last item the players put on is their helmet.

The goalkeepers need some extra protection and as a result wear strong leg guards, a chest-protector, a face mask and extra-padded gloves.

Ice hockey boots are rather different from those used for figure skating inasmuch as they have lower internal supports, along with protective toe and heel caps, moulded arch supports and tendon-protectors. The blade is rather narrow and reinforced by hollow tubing. The goalkeeper wears a wider, yet lower blade to enhance his balance. His blades also have additional posts to prevent the puck passing between the top of the blade and the bottom of the boot.

The ice hockey rink

The ideal size for a hockey rink is about the same as is used for major international figure-skating competitions, sixty-one metres in length by thirty metres in width.

The edges of the ice are marked by a wooden or plastic barrier, otherwise known as the boards, which is approximately four feet high. The boards are topped by either a plexi-glass screen or netting to protect the spectators and to keep the puck in play at all times.

The ice is marked in such a way as to divide up the playing surface in the following manner. Red goal lines are drawn some ten feet from each end of the rink. The goals, which are 1.22 metres in height and 1.83 metres in width, are placed centrally along these lines.

The goals have integral nets to contain the puck in the event of a goal. For safety reasons they are not fixed in any way to the ice.

The rink is divided into three areas or zones by two blue lines. Running across the centre of the rink between the two blue lines is a red line. The centre of the rink is located by a blue spot enclosed within a large blue circle, thirty feet in diameter.

There are also four red circles, two in each half, which are placed at a point fifteen feet from the goal, between each goal post and the barrier. These are known as the face-off spots. Along side each of these face-off spots, there are red lines, sixty centimetres in length, running parallel to the goal lines. There are additional red lines ninety centimetres in length which run from the outer edge of all four red circles.

In the centre zone there are two red spots, placed at a distance of five feet from each blue line, midway between the side barriers.

The game

There are two referees for amateur matches, one for each half of the ice, whereas in N.H.L. matches there is only one referee along with two linesmen. Their main duty is to point out off-sides using a whistle.

Canada versus USSR

A game of ice hockey lasts for sixty minutes, divided into three periods of twenty minutes. The minutes are only counted when the puck is in play. Although only six players on each side are allowed on the ice at any particular time, substitutes may be introduced whenever the teams feel the necessity. The teams keep quite a few players on hand ready for substitution when needed.

The first stage in a game of ice hockey, involves a 'face-off' and this occurs when the referee drops the puck on to the ice in the centre of the rink, between the sticks of the centremen from each team. A face-off also occurs when some kind of misplay takes place. Under these circumstances, the face-off will take place on the nearest marked spot on the ice surface. The puck becomes 'dead' only when it is hit over the barrier or in the event of an infringement.

There are goal judges situated so that they can switch on a red light behind the relevant goal in the event of a goal being scored. A goal can only be scored using a stick. The goal will not be counted in the event of an opposing player being in the relevant goal crease.

The two blue lines divide the playing area into three zones. These are **defence, neutral** and **attacking**. The defence zone corresponds to the area nearest your own goal. The neutral zone corresponds to the central area of the ice and the attacking refers to that closest to your opponents' goal.

The puck must enter the attacking zone in advance of the player.

Rough play is penalized by way of the offender being sent to sit in the penalty box, at the side of the rink, for two minutes or more, depending on what crime has been committed.

20 *Ice Skating as a Career*

This chapter covers the career opportunities open to reasonably high-standard ice skaters. The first sections cover those relating to the figure skaters, the latter part refers to careers in ice hockey and arena management.

Show skating

When figure skaters finish their competitive careers, it is usual for them to consider the options open to them, which amount to skating in shows, or coaching.

The top championship skaters often take up show contracts with one of the big ice shows, such as 'Holiday on Ice', 'Ice Capades', or 'Ice Follies'. The champions are highly sought after, as their skating will draw the crowds in to see the show. But there are also openings for other skaters who are sufficiently skilled, of the correct height, physical appearance and age.

Therefore should you become a great name in the sport, the world will be at your feet; not only will the ice shows want you, but you will also be invited to take part in television shows and offered advertising work. Your name and recommendation will be sufficient to sell the relevant product. In fact all kinds of career opportunities will fall at your feet.

For those of you who are not quite so famous, the ice shows still need you to back up the chorus. There are always many openings for the right skaters and auditions are held in major European and North American cities.

The shows travel from place to place and from country to country, so it really is a great way to see the world for a couple of years and be paid for your time and effort.

There are many ice shows touring on the European and North American continents. Some companies travel to the Far East too.

Each of these companies will travel for many months, moving from city to city. Each show will have a portable ice rink known as a tank which enables the refrigeration engineers to set up an ice rink very quickly just about anywhere.

Torvill and Dean, the ultimate ice dancers, in one of their touring ice shows

The big names will be required to star in one of these touring companies for a certain mutually agreed period.

Some of the best-known skaters have organized their own independent shows, usually starring themselves.

If you are a particularly good free skater without being a great name, there is still the possibility of becoming a star, by starting out as an understudy for someone who is a star. If the star is unable to skate, you will have your big chance. You may even be able to create an act by getting a partner and working out a clever routine.

If you would like to be part of this action, there are several things of which you must be aware. Firstly, you must realistically assess your skating skills and secondly, you must be of good physical shape and appearance. If you are overweight, the company will require you to diet until your appearance is reasonable. There is also an acceptable height range along with minimum skating-skill requirements.

Before going to your audition, you would be well advised to go and see a few shows and assess the standard of the chorus and then make sure that you are able to skate any move that you see them perform. You must be capable of performing high-standard spirals (arabesques), and also of jumping and spinning to a pretty high standard.

When you join the show you will be required to attend numerous rehearsals in order to learn the various routines and harmonize with the other members of the cast.

Professional coaching

In Canada

Many skaters turn professional and teach others. Before you are able to do this, you must have attained a high test level as it is only reasonable that you should be of a really high standard before being set loose on the general public.

In many countries, including Canada, professional coaches are required to undertake further training, rather like a teacher's, in order to standardize the level of teaching nationally. This is a great way of ensuring competence amongst the trainers.

Canada is dominated by the national sport, ice hockey, which competes with figure skating for ice practice time.

Most skating coaches work on a free-lance, self-employed basis, contracting their services to as many people or ice rinks as they need to earn their income. As a rule, professionals work for several clubs and this, naturally enough, involves a great deal of travelling. (One year, I worked for seven clubs!) This is because it is difficult to get enough ice time in any one place and even the smallest community will have its arena with many different demands being made upon it by the locals. (Figure skating may not be the priority.)

As with most self-employed occupations, professional coaches are only paid for the work that they do, so they receive no support during illness or holiday periods. However, some clubs do pay their professionals a retainer, simply for being available to work for them and for giving this commitment.

Professional coaches are paid in several different ways. Firstly, for club lessons (this includes groups of children, adults, tiny tots, stroking and power skating), there will be an agreed hourly rate paid to the professional by the club.

You will be required to invoice the treasurer, who will give you a cheque for the amount owed. You will also teach private lessons for more advanced skaters who need individual attention to perfect their skills. They will be directly responsible for meeting their fee obligations to you. Again, you will have to bill them, unless you have a different agreed method of obtaining payment. If you have difficulty getting your fees, the clubs will usually try to help you do so. You will not usually pay any percentage of your earnings to the club.

The Canadian skating season is highly dependent upon ice hockey as this factor generally determines when the rinks have their ice. This means that for approximately six months there will be ice time (between late September and early April).

After this time the professional figure-skating coaches must either organize a spring school or find a convenient rink which is running one and take their pupils to this. Spring schools generally run for four or five weeks until the first or second week in May, after which time the ice is taken up.

Summer schools run for between six and eight weeks and there is usually one in the region, but certainly not in every town. There is a break at the end of summer school for a few weeks until fall school in early September. Fall school runs straight into winter school.

In the United Kingdom

In the United Kingdom, it is usual for a professional to work for only one ice rink, whereas in Canada that would be unusual. There has always been a shortage of high-level skating coaches and as the skating 'market' in the United Kingdom has doubled as we enter the nineties, continued expansion seems likely. Therefore the demand for coaches seems likely to increase too.

The skating season runs all year, so there is not usually the need to travel to different rinks to make your living.

Another factor to consider is that many rinks in the United Kingdom are privately operated, without any kind of state or local-authority grant, and as a result depend on receiving as much income as possible to meet their outgoings.

Many rinks have a 'lesson' desk or office where people can book their lessons, paying for them in advance. The rinks will take some kind of commission, usually in the form of a percentage from the professional in order to cover the cost of this service and for the right to use the rink to make their living.

Alternatively some rinks work on a system whereby the professional pays an agreed ice rental and then collects his fees directly from the pupil, as in the Canadian system mentioned above. It should be stressed that if you are highly qualified or a big name in the sport, you may be able to negotiate a more advantageous rate.

In the United Kingdom, the majority of ice dancers attempting N.S.A. tests will be partnered by professional coaches. This is simply because they are generally excellent ice dancers with great experience and probably will have taught the candidate as well.

Professional ice hockey players

The great stars of ice hockey do really have the world at their feet; in fact, these are the people who can almost write their own pay cheque.

It goes without saying that great talent and skill are needed as well as the good luck and ambition to make it. So work hard and you never know . . .

Ice rink/arena managers

For those of you who wish to promote and organize the skating within the rinks, with or without actually teaching or skating, there is always the possibility of becoming an ice supervisor or manager.

It must be said that this is an extremely demanding job, often involving working long and anti-social hours. But the leisure industry is growing so quickly that the future looks bright for those with the relevant skills, personality and drive.

SUMMARY

This chapter deals with the prospects of making a living as a professional in the ice-skating business.

The first section deals with show skating and tells

you in detail how to join up, along with the age, physical and skating requirements.

The second section deals with teaching ice skating as an occupation. The skating qualifications required are high, and there is always a shortage of good coaches.

The varying systems for professionals working in Canada and the United Kingdom are contrasted. In Canada it is the norm to work for several clubs and travel to wherever there is sufficient ice time, as the sport is seasonally based. In the United Kingdom, the work is all-year-round.

The next section deals with some more financial stars of the skating world, the top professional ice hockey players. There is a fantastic career ahead for those with sufficient talent and good fortune, although the physical demands are extremely high.

The last section is for those people who would like to move into ice rink management. With the necessary administrative skills and skating knowledge, this shouldn't be a problem.

21 *Ice Skating as a Spectator Sport*

If you have children, grandchildren or even an enthusiastic partner who skates, surely it would be a good idea for you to become involved in some capacity with the sport.

This doesn't mean you have to skate yourself. I am concentrating this section on providing information as to how to become involved and informed without taking to the ice.

Statistically, ice skating is one of the most popular viewing sports amongst women at this moment and yet many of them may never have skated in their lives. The inspirational appeal of the sport remains even so and I plan to show you how to increase your general knowledge of the sport, in order to help you to enjoy watching it more.

Every year the major championships are shown on television and an excellent commentary is provided to fill in any gaps in skating knowledge — as not everybody knows a triple axel when they see one!

Watch and listen and you soon will recognize one from a triple salchow. It is a good idea to tape the various programmes and play them back a few times, so that you get a good idea of what individual moves look like. You will soon learn to identify these jumps and spins even when they are performed by other people. Although many moves look the same, to the experienced eye, they are all quite different.

If your children are involved in the sport and are still quite young, most probably they will want you to sit near the edge, watching and encouraging their every move. This is great and so important in the development of their enthusiasm and therefore their skating skills.

So get your woollen blanket out and head off to the rink with your children (don't forget your thermos with a warm drink inside).

Becoming involved will enable you to learn the system operating in your rink. You will need to find out about such areas as the best practice times, patch sessions and free ice availability. You must also find out about the proficiency tests available to encourage progress, since the only way you can find out is to be there and ask loads of questions.

Your child's skating professional is generally a mine of information and the best place to start, so don't be afraid of asking questions, no matter how trivial they seem. A professional will most certainly understand that you must be kept informed concerning relevant areas, e.g. your child's progress, expectations that can be reasonably fulfilled and tests that must be worked for and attempted. You will also need to know how many lessons and practice sessions are needed and when and where any relevant skating competitions are to take place.

Don't overlook the fact that it will be up to you to sort out and send off any entry forms and you may also be required to transport your child to the competition rink.

By now I hope that you can see the importance of your role and how necessary any knowledge of the workings of the sport will be to you.

When your children are practising, video their moves from time to time so that they can judge their own progress realistically. They may be surprised how they look and can gain a great deal from the experience, learning to criticize their moves or gain encouragement from their progress.

For those of you in Canada there is another area in which volunteers are required. There is always a great shortage of judges and it should be noted that previous skating knowledge or experience is not always necessary to become a judge. You will be trained to look for certain errors and award marks according to the moves that are performed correctly. When you have attended sufficient training seminars and have also trial-judged on the required number of occasions, you will become a judge of that particular level.

You will then undertake more training, seminars and so on, until you are considered to be sufficiently competent to be able to judge at the next level.

The skating clubs are always in great need of helpful volunteers. If you have a specific skill, such as accountancy, there is always a place for your services, and they will be greatly appreciated.

There is also a shortage of D.J.'s to announce and play the skaters' programme music. Most of the parents take turns and you could too.

As for the hockey players, they too need a great deal of support and dedication from their families and friends.

How many people are prepared to get up at the crack of dawn in order to take their children down to the rink for a hockey practice? And this could be many times each week.

You need to be seriously interested in the sport to be able to perform these services without resentment. So, if your kid wants to make it into his local team, or even higher, get involved and provide the support he needs. Get involved.

Without the parental support, ice hockey could never find its up-and-coming new players.

So parents, grandparents and friends of skating, get involved. The sport needs you!

22 General Information

The purpose of this chapter is to fill in a little background information with regard to general fitness, various skating systems, test structures and such issues as the experience of your first competition and whether you could ever become a champion.

The first area that I am going to cover is that of general physical fitness.

How fit do I need to be?

Before venturing out on to the ice, you would be well advised to get yourself into good physical shape.

Adults need to be more aware of this area than do the children. The parts of your body that are going to take most of the strain are your legs and feet. To give yourself sufficient stamina, you need whole-body fitness and there are various ways that this can be achieved. You can take exercise classes and/or you can get your local fitness centre to devise a programme of weights, etc., specifically to aid those areas of the body most relevant to ice skating.

Many people find cycling a good exercise for skating as both activities require a pushing action of the legs.

Dance classes can be a useful way of getting into shape for both sexes. They will help your posture too!

If you carry more weight than you should, this is not going to be advantageous for several reasons. Firstly, you will have more body weight to move than most people, and this could lead to disappointment when jumping. Secondly, your appearance is never going to be as good as the slimmer person's. When you consider that ice skating is heavily artistically dependent on physical appearance, additional weight is only going to be a disadvantage.

How do the test systems work?

In the United Kingdom and most other countries where ice skating is reasonably advanced, there are detailed test systems covering all aspects of the sport.

It is usual to start with a preliminary test which amounts to an introduction to the test system and work through towards gold.

In the free-skating sections there are various lists of jumps and spins that must be successfully completed, followed by skating routines of varying length and difficulty according to the test being attempted.

The ice-dance tests require the candidate to skate with a partner, at the lower levels various compulsory dances along with a solo of one of these. This may be followed by a variation dance. For the higher tests, the skater will be required to skate several parts to his or her tests. This means there will be numerous compulsory dances followed by an original-rhythm dance and a free dance.

The pair skating tests are run along similar lines to the free skating with certain set elements followed by routines of different lengths according to the tests being attempted.

Although the compulsory figures have taken a much lower profile these days the tests still exist. Each level has certain specified figures that must be skated.

Could I ever become a champion?

There are many different things that are required of a champion. The first area that I would like to cover is that of the age of the skater.

The current standard of skating in all its forms is so high that any future champions will have to be able to perform all the moves done at the present time along with many more advanced elements, perhaps as yet unseen. This means that the skaters of the future will have to be able to learn all their triple and quadruple jumps as early as possible.

If a young child of perhaps five years of age is able to enjoy and work hard at skating along with having ability, motivation and financial backing, he or she may well get close to the top. Along with the aforementioned requirements comes an element of luck — you must be in the right place at the right time. This could mean that some years there is less competition than in others. This can sometimes be true of the competitive year following the Olympic Games, when many of the big names retire, leaving space for others to advance up the ranking.

Charles Wildridge, one of Britain's senior international competitors, in the middle of a great jump

How the skating clubs work

In Canada

In Canada, most towns have figure-skating clubs. These clubs hire ice time from the 'arena' (ice rink) for the exclusive use of their members. This ice time is allocated generally according to the size of the club membership and the total demand made by all potential arena users. As there is a great deal of competition from ice hockey, this is the most reasonable way to sort things out.

The skating clubs are run by private individuals, usually the parents of current skaters, on a non-profit basis. Any additional money earned by the club is put towards future ice-rental costs. Sometimes, depending on the local authority, the clubs are able to get subsidies towards the cost of their ice time. This means that they will have to pay a lower rate per hour than if they were hiring the ice on a one-off basis and can lower the individual cost of membership.

The Canadian Figure Skating Association (address in the appendix) keeps full records of all the clubs in Canada and would be the best place to start if you need to know where the clubs are, who is the best person to call, etc.

In the United Kingdom

In the United Kingdom the set up is slightly different. In effect the ice rinks fill the same role as the Canadian skating clubs. The U.K. clubs try to offer their members a few hours each week (the rink provides the majority of practice hours) for their exclusive use. It is usual for competing skaters to represent a skating club.

In the rink you will usually find a club notice board which will give you contact information. Call the club secretary and find out such basics as operating times, membership requirements and cost. The ice rink should also be able to give advice regarding club sessions, etc.

For a full list of skating clubs, contact the National

Skating Association, whose address is in the appendix at the back of this book.

The ice show

The high point of the skating season is the ice show. Bearing this in mind all good ice rinks make a serious effort to make this as much fun and as entertaining as possible.

There is room for skaters of all standards and age groups, but it must be said that few things could be more appealing than the sight of a small child skating or even wobbling across the rink covered in feathers or some other outrageous costume.

Practices start a couple of months prior to the big day and it is usual for these to be organized by the professional coaches.

Generally, each coach agrees to choreograph a line number, often including many of his or her pupils.

Various sorts of show may be staged, varying from pantomime to children's parties, which include various routines as part of the entertainment.

Ice pantomimes require a good deal of time and effort, ranging from organizing the script to arranging for people to act as the voices for the miming ice skaters.

In the snowy regions of the United States and Canada it is usual for each town to hold a winter skating carnival.

Should you or your child wish to be involved with these ice spectaculars, make your number known to the organizers, who are generally either the local ice rink management or skating coaches.

When you have done so, you will be informed as to when the practices/rehearsals are to be held.

Naturally being part of these shows requires a good deal of dedication from the participants. This means that you must be available and reliable concerning the necessary practices.

The dress rehearsal

As show time approaches, it is usual to have a couple of dress rehearsals. These involve running through the whole production to music, with all participants wearing their relevant costumes. This is generally the time when mistakes can be eradicated.

The big night

This is the time when there is frenetic activity, with all the mums dressing up their children, and the make-up and hairdressing experts on hand to apply the finishing touches.

You may be pleasantly surprised how well the show goes on the night, as everybody pulls together, fired by the charge of having a really enthusiastic audience. This appreciation is the payback for all the hard work that has been put into the production.

Do offer your services to the organizers of the local ice show, even if it isn't on the performance side. As you can imagine, help is needed in every conceivable area, from costume-making to playing the music and, of course, promoting the show, so get involved and have fun!

23 *Glossary of Skating Terms*

BACKWARD OUTSIDE CURVE – A skating movement which occurs when the skater is moving backward on an outside edge

BACKWARD INSIDE EDGE – A skating movement which occurs when the skater is moving backwards on an inside edge

BARRIER/BOARDS – The low wooden or plastic wall marking the edge of the ice surface and which surrounds the rink

CANASTA TANGO – Compulsory dance set to a tango rhythm

CENTRE – The starting and also meeting point of circles in compulsory figures

CHANGE OF EDGE/SERPENTINE – A skating movement which involves starting on a particular edge and changing to the other edge, without changing foot

CHASSE – Two steps travelling on the same curve, consisting of an outside, then an inside. It is usual to repeat the first step

COMPULSORY DANCES – Set sequences of steps which interpret a particular character of dance and performed by all skaters without any variation of the footwork

COMPULSORY FIGURES – Skating in such a way in order to produce circles on the ice surface

CROSSOVERS/CROSSCUTS BACKWARD – A backward outside stroke made by crossing the free foot over in front of the skating foot

CROSSOVERS/CROSSCUTS FORWARD — A forward outside stroke made by crossing the free foot over in front of the skating foot

THE DIP — A move which involves standing with the feet together, then bending the knees until it is possible to touch the underneath of the skating boots

DOUBLE TRACKING — When both skates are on the ice for longer than is necessary to make the push

DRAG — A movement whereby the skater bends down low on the skating knee, stretching the free leg back and dragging the free foot along the ice

DUTCH WALTZ — Compulsory dance set to a waltz rhythm

EDGE — The cutting edge of the skate

FLAT — When the skate is held perpendicular, both edges are in contact with the ice at the same time

FREE DANCE — A skating programme devised by a dance couple, performed in order to interpret several different musical tempos and lasting for a set time period

FORWARD GLIDE — A skating movement which occurs when the skater is moving forwards on one foot

ICE RINK/ICE PAD — The skating area

INSIDE EDGE — The edge of the blade which corresponds to the inside of the particular foot

KILIAN HOLD — This is a hold in ice dancing when both parties are facing in the same direction, standing hip to hip

LONG FREE PROGRAMME — A free-skating programme of a specified length which forms the last and major part of singles free-skating championships

MOHAWK — A 180-degree turn from either forwards or backwards, which involves changing feet but not the subsequent edge

ORIGINAL-RHYTHM DANCE — A dance devised by each couple in a competition set to a particular character and rhythm. It has a fixed length and cannot include any lifts, but can include two different pieces of music

OUTSIDE EDGE — The edge of the skate that corresponds to the outside of the particular foot

PAIR SKATING — Two people skating together in such a way as to produce lifts, pair spins, and free skating in harmony with each other

PATCH — An area of ice reserved for practising compulsory figures. This is usually an area of clean ice so that the skater's tracings may be studied

PATTERN — The design on the ice surface made by a dance or any other movements in free or pair skating

PRELIMINARY FOXTROT — A compulsory dance set to a foxtrot rhythm

PROGRESSIVE — A series of steps on a curve, outside and inside edges alternatively

RUN — See progressive

SCRIBE — A device used to mark and measure compulsory figures

SHORT FREE PROGRAMME — A free-skating programme of a specified length which includes compulsory movements

SKATING FOOT — The foot on which you are standing

SKATE GUARDS — Plastic or rubber blade-protectors

SNOW PLOUGH — A method of stopping on the ice. See Chapter 6

SPIRAL — A position which can be performed on any edge whereby the body is held nearly horizontal, with the free leg in line with the body. (Sometimes called an arabesque.)

STROKE — A step on to an edge, which involves an increase of speed

STROKING — The usual method of forward propulsion

THREE JUMP/WALTZ JUMP — A jump which involves taking off on a forward outside edge on one foot and landing backwards on the other foot also on an outside edge, having made a 180-degree turn

THREE TURN — A turn from either forwards to

backwards or backwards to forwards, which involves a change of edge but no change of foot. See Chapter 10

TOE PICKS — The sharp serrated area at the front of the skate

TOE PUSHING — When the skater uses the picks to push

TRACING — The mark left on the ice by the skate

TRAILING — When the free foot drags along on the ice when it should be raised

T STOP — A method of stopping

Appendix I

List of U.K. ice rinks

Greater London

Alexandra Palace, Wood Green, London N22 4AY
Tel 081-365 2121

Broadgate Ice, Liverpool Street, London EC2
Tel 071-588 6565

Lee Valley Ice Rink, Lea Bridge Road, London E10 7QL
Tel 081-533 3151

Queens Ice Skating Club, Queensway, London W2 4QP
Tel 071-229 0172

Richmond Ice Rink, Clevedon Road, Twickenham, Middlesex TW1 2HX
Tel 081-892 3646 − Possibly closing 1991/2

Sobell Centre, Hornsey Road, Islington, London N7
Tel 071-607 1643

Streatham Ice Rink, 386 Streatham High Road, London SW16 6HT
Tel 081-769 7771

South East

Gillingham Ice Rink, Gillingham, Kent
Tel 0634 388477

Sussex Ice Rink, Queens Square, Brighton
Tel 0273 24677

East Midlands

Nottingham Ice Stadium, Lower Parliament Street,
Nottingham
Tel 0602 51938

Sutton Ice Centre, High Pavement, Sutton-in-Ashfield,
Nottinghamshire
Tel 0623 554554

West Midlands

Solihull Ice Rink, Hobbs Moat Road, Solihull
Tel 021-724 4315

Telford Ice Rink, Telford Town Centre, Telford TF3
4JQ
Tel 0952 291511

Eastern Region

Blade Runner Ice Arena, Milton Keynes Leisure Park,
1 South Row, Childs Way, Milton Keynes MK9 1BL

Riverside Ice & Leisure Centre, Chelmsford CM1 1FG
Tel 0245 269417

Romford Valley Ice Rink, Rom Valley Way, Romford
RM7 OAF
Tel 0708 24734

Stevenage Ice Bowl, Roaring Meg Leisure Park,
Stevenage, Hertfordshire
Tel 0488 740750

North West Region

Altrincham Ice Rink, Devonshire Road, Altrincham,
Cheshire
Tel 061-928 1360

Blackburn Arena, Lower Audley, Blackburn, Lan-
cashire

Blackpool Ice Drome, South Shore, Blackpool
Tel 0253 41707

Northern Region

Forum Ice Rink, Town Centre, Billingham
Tel 0642 554449

Crowtree Leisure Centre, Sunderland
Tel 091-514 2511

Durham Ice Rink, Walkergate, Durham
Tel 0385 64065

Whitley Bay Ice Rink, Hill Heads Road, Whitley Bay
Tel 0632 526240

Southern Region

Aldershot Ice Rink, Pool Road, Aldershot, Hampshire
Tel 0252 336464

Basingstoke Ice Rink, West Ham Park, Basingstoke,
Hampshire RG22 6PG
Tel 0256 840219

John Nike Leisuresport Complex, Bracknell, Berkshire
RG12 4TH
Tel 0344 860033

Oxford Ice Rink, Oxpens Road, Oxford
Tel 0865 248076

Slough Ice Arena, Monten Lane, Slough, Berkshire
Tel 0753 821555

South West Region

Bristol Ice Rink, Frogmore Street, Bristol 1
Tel 0272 292148

Bournemouth Ice Rink, Hinton Road, Bournemouth,
Dorset BH1 2EN
Tel 0202 293011

Swindon Ice Rink, Link Centre, Westlea, Swindon,
Wiltshire
Tel 0793 871212

Gosport Ice Rink, Forest Way, Fairham Road,
Gosport, Hampshire PQ13 OZX
Tel 0705 511217

Yorkshire & Humberside

Grimsby Leisure Centre, Cromwell Road, South Humberside
Tel 0472 242000

Humberside Ice Arena, Kingston Street, Hull, North
Humberside
Tel 0482 25252

Bradford Ice Arena, Little Horton Lane, Bradford
Tel 0274 733535

Sheffield Ice Arena, Queens Road, Sheffield
Tel 0742 23037

Wales

Deeside Leisure Centre, Deeside, Clwyd
Tel 0244 812311

Wales National Ice Rink, Hayesbridge Road, Cardiff
CF1 3GH
Tel 0222 383451

Scotland

Aviemore Centre Ice Rink,
Tel 0479 810624

Ayr Ice Rink, 9 Limekiln Road, Ayr KA8 8DG
Tel 0292 263024

The Auchenhavie Centre, Saltcoats Road, Stevenson,
Ayrshire KA20 3JR

Dundee-Angus Ice Rink, Kingsway West, Dundee
Tel 0382 825222

Murrayfield Ice Rink, Riverside Crescent, Edinburgh
Tel 031-337 6933

Summit Centre Ice Rink, Minerva Way, Glasgow
Tel 041-204 2215

Lanarkshire Ice Rink, Hamilton
Tel 0698 282448

Inverness Ice Centre, Bught Park, Inverness
0463 235711

Magnum Leisure Centre, Irvine, Ayrshire
Tel 0294 78381

Border Ice Rink, Abbotseat Road, Kelso
Tel 0573 24774

The Galleon Centre, Titchfield Street, Kilmarnock,
Ayrshire

Kirkaldy Ice Rink, Rosslyn Street, Kirkaldy, Fife
Tel 0592 52151

Lockerbie Ice Rink, Glasgow Road, Lockerbie
Tel 05762 2197

Central Scotland Ice Rink, Williamsfield, Stirling
Tel 0738 24188

Northern Ireland

Crystals Arena, Castle Park Road, Bangor, Co. Down

Dundonald International Ice Bowl, Old Dundonald,
Co. Down
Tel 02318 2611

Appendix II: Skating Events – National and International

United Kingdom:

Primary (Novice) Championships (mens, ladies, pairs and dance)

Junior Championships (mens, ladies, pairs and dance)

Senior Championships (mens, ladies, pairs and dance)

Canada:

Novice Championships (mens, ladies, pairs and dance)

Junior Championships (mens, ladies, pairs and dance)

Senior Championships (mens, ladies, pairs and dance)

European Championships:

Mens, ladies, pairs and dance

World Championships:

Mens, ladies, pairs and dance

Olympic Games

Mens, ladies, pairs and dance

Appendix III: Skating Organizations and Equipment Suppliers

Skating Organizations

National Skating Association of Great Britain (figure
and free skating, dance, pairs and speed)
15—17 Gee Street
London EC1V 3RE
Tel 071-253 3824/0910

Canadian Figure Skating Association
1600 James Naismith Drive
Gloucester, Ontario KIB 5N4
Canada

United States Figure Skating Association
20 First Street
Colorado Springs
Co 80906
U.S.A.

International Skating Union
Haus Schoneck
Promenade 73
Postfach
CH-7270
Davos-Platz
Switzerland

Equipment suppliers and distributors

John Wilson, Marsden Bros & Co. (blade
manufacturers)
71 Greystock Street
Sheffield S47 WA
U.K.

D & A (Leisure) (all ice skating equipment, U.K. and
overseas)
20 Wimpole Street
London W1
United Kingdom
Tel 071-243 8161

Acknowledgements

Denise Taylor, for taking many of the photographs. Sandra Gatehouse (illustrations). Vanessa Riley (judging section). Adrienne de Mont. Belinda Bucknall QC, for many great ideas. Nigel Robinson, for introducing me to Transworld. Debbie Beckerman, for her advice and help. Andrew Gooding, for moral support. Betty Loach, for checking the ice dance section. John Presland (Managing Director, Queens Ice Club), for old skating photographs and use of the rink. Gerry Groves, old skating photographs. Tom and Enid Taylor, for their help and support. Eric Bogg, (Managing Director, John Wilson, Marsden Bros and Co), skate photographs and manufacturing advice. Courtney Jones OBE, for much help, advice and information. National Skating Association of Great Britain, (skating facts and figures). Canadian Figure Skating Association. Barbara Wilson, PR, Canadian Figure Skating Association (for permission to reproduce part of the Canskate Program). Kay Robinson (precision skating). Mike and Jenny Smith, Lea Valley Ice Centre (help with ice hockey and precision). Diane Herman (entertainment). Alexis, Dino and Theo Dimopoulos, Shereen Hussein, Jamie Spiteri, John and Lisa Dunn, for taking part in photographic sessions.

Joan Slater and John Goding, for teaching me to skate.

Picture Credits

Allsport pp. 104, 149; AllSport/Tony Duffy pp. 129, 159; Allsport/
Bob Martin pp. 11, 100, 146, 148, 150; AllSport/Mike Powell p. 164;
AllSport/Steve Powell p.161; Eric Bogg pp. 38, 39, 40; Campbell's
Press Studio p.16; J. Stamp p. 127; Alex Morton p. 131; National
Skating Association of GB p. 154; Pic Photos p. 46; Mike Smith p.
132; Denise Taylor pp. 9, 13, 23, 34, 42, 72, 81, 118, 119; John
Webster p. 175.

Line drawings by Sandra Gatehouse.